BETWEEN MY ROCK & SOME HARD PLACES

BETWEEN MY ROCK & SOME HARD PLACES

CLEVROY "DEPO" DEPRADINE

Copyright © 2024 by Clevroy "Depo" DePradine.

Library of Congress Control Number: 2024903807
ISBN: Hardcover   979-8-3694-1197-1
        Softcover   979-8-3694-1196-4
        eBook   979-8-3694-1682-2

All rights reserved. No part of this book may be reproduced or transmitted in any form or by any means, electronic or mechanical, including photocopying, recording, or by any information storage and retrieval system, without permission in writing from the copyright owner.

Any people depicted in stock imagery provided by Getty Images are models, and such images are being used for illustrative purposes only. Certain stock imagery © Getty Images.

Photo credits and compliments:

Front cover Photo: Betty DePradine
Foreword: Professor Ronald "Pappy" Charles
Evelyn Ross
Anthony Windell DeRiggs, George Johnson, Clarence Medford, Rawle Steele, Fitzpatrick Belgrave, Leonard Noel, Michael "Smico" Marryshow, Darryl Brathwaite, Clyde Viechweg, Karl Otway, James Clarkson, Cheryl Fletcher, Stokely Phillip, Pat "Adams" Nicholson.

Photos: Easter Water Parade (Mr. Graham).
Photo: "Hell Cats" (National Geographic).
Federal Maple and Federal Palm: Stevenson Manners
Back cover: Sylvester Photography

Printed in the United States of America

Rev. date: 02/28/2024

To order additional copies of this book, contact:
Xlibris
844-714-8691
www.Xlibris.com
Orders@Xlibris.com
855458

Photo credits: Depo

Panoramic view of "the Wharf" (Rawle Steele).

Foreword

Writing is hard—even for authors who do it all the time. Less frequent practitioners—the graduate students with thesis proposals; job applicants; executives with annual reports; the child writing to Santa Claus to request that special gift—often get stuck in an awkward passage or have challenges finding descriptive words, and then they blame themselves. What should be easy and flowing looks tangled, feeble, or overblown—and not what was meant at all. That's definitely not the case with Clevroy "Depo" DePradine's *Between My Rock and Some Hard Places*, which is an excellent read. He hit the ball out of the park and touched all the bases during his home run trot.

Clevroy did a masterful job of weaving the tale. He used metaphorical terms as he developed the characters enough to bring them to life, and he shared enough detail to bring the reader in close without being wordy or boring.

His story began with a tribute to his father, Aubrey "Paddy" DePradine. He pointedly made reference to his Cooper Hill community and his times in Hindsey School. He proudly reminded the reader of his pan-playing days with Angel Harps Steel Orchestra and "liming" under Empire Cinema (the sheltered area at the front of the building) on the Wharf (commonly known as the Carenage).

The book of chatter tales and life experiences entered my soul, heart, blood, and flesh, right from the very first line. It is a revelation—a read of an engaging and captivating caliber. Further venturing into Depo's reservoir of information, I became curious about the special formula he employed, which makes every single line smile with a breathtaking quality. A silent cultural undercurrent continues to throb underneath his every line, rewarding the reader with a sublime experience of spiritual enrichment and gratifying humor. He skillfully conveys the harsh realities and stays in step with the more serious trends of the times.

Coping with life's brutality and a steady stream of contradictory information can be debilitating, but Depo invites you to momentarily switch off your mind from the distractions and coast through the satirical underpinnings of his must-read story!

Ronald "Pappy" Charles

Acknowledgments

I dedicate this book to the memory of my dad, Aubrey Gore "Paddy" DePradine, who left us in the year of the Lord 1970. He was a humble, quiet, hardworking man who gave much of himself with the little he had in his relatively short time on earth. To my mom, Christiana (Chrissie), who made enormous sacrifices to provide for her children amid the hardships after the passing of my dad.

Thanks to my family: my wife, Betty, who encouraged me to stop telling stories and write, my sons, Khary and Tereek, and my little spark of a grandson, Austin. To all those who were there when I found myself wedged between my rock and some very hard places. Special mention and thanks to Rosalind "Baby" Greenidge (may her soul rest in peace) and Donna LaTouche and her family who offered me a second home and helped me to collect the shattered pieces during one of the most difficult and challenging periods of my life.

Angel Harps as an institution for providing a clef in the rock where I was able to deposit my frustrations (not in a bin but in my pan). And most importantly, the Almighty is my sure refuge of strength. All who encouraged me to annotate the stories of our collective experiences to be stored in our archives for preservation and reflections. Special thanks to my brother Lincoln "Toro" DePradine, Anthony Windell DeRiggs, and Sandra Antoine Cespedes for their invaluable assistance.

Professor Ronald "Pappy" Charles for taking the time to elucidate and validate this transcript. Extended family and friends for their promptings, challenges, and encouragement that have now come to fruition. My former coworkers: Dorice, who constantly chastised me, Sharon, and my former supervisor, Brenda Hannah for her mentorship. The aged stalwarts of Carroll Street and Rawle Steele for surrendering his home when we needed a man-cave to reminisce with satisfied stomachs.

This book is not intended to compete but to complement those who have persevered in preserving and providing the valuable memories and moments that positively molded us. This collective package is for posterity; I hope others will complete this experience, this journey, and this remarkable community called "the Wharf."

Thanks to each and every one of you for your encouragement and support.

Contents

Foreword vii
Acknowledgments ix

Aubrey "Paddy" DePradine: Cooper's Hill 1
Tant Cho Cho 9
The Hill and the Standpipe: Where More than Water Flowed 10
The Steps 20
The Hill, the People, and Their Politics 22
Eric Matthew Gairy: The Man, His Mystique, and His Mission 24
Ogilvie House and the Big Stones: A Mystery Never Solved 27
School, Community, and Class 30
Introduction to the Wharf Community 39
The Wharf: A Tourist Delight 47
Bianca C: The Wharf to the Rescue 51
University of Empire: An Institution Called Angel Harps 53
From the Cinema Screen to the CID 55
The Wharf by Night 58
It Was Here on the Wharf 60
Brofitt Shop and Marshall Shop 62
Under Empire 64
Mas and Laugh 66
The Character and the Characters from the Wharf 68
The Day Grubay Became Easter Water Parade MC 73
Nurse Radix: "The Deliverer" 77
The Man: Leon (Tomkeen) 79
The Women from the Wharf Who Made A Difference 81
Miss Omega 82

Mammy Fletch	83
Roslind "Baby" Greenidge	84
Pamela "Pam" Steele	85
Empire: The Glory Days of House, Pit, Balcony, and Box	87
The Classics	90
Pan in We Blood	93
George Croney's Split with Angel Harps	103
Panasonic (David) Goes Up against Angel Harps (Goliath)	107
Sons of the Brave	113
Angel Harps Loses Panorama and Band of the Year - Walter "Dictator" Thomas captures Calypso Title (69)	117
Arthur Bowen and Angel Harps: Man on a Mission or a Mercenary	120
Two Rebels in White	122
A Bold Move: The Saints and the Scoundrels	124
The Makings of an Album: Brighter Out of Darkness	132
Maestros: James "Wakax" Clarkson and Lester Boyke	138
The Night Ugly Sam Left Us Standing	142
The Many Faces of James "Wakax" Clarkson	145
Keith "Keithy" Rougier	150
Another Angel Harps Member Made It on the Big Stage as a Drummer	152
The Iron and the Iron Men	155
Angel Harps: Their Flagmen/Women, Engine Room, and Supporters	157
Steelband Men and Nicknames	159
Unique Arrangements and Awards	162
Sailing into Uncharted Waters	171
The Year the Flamingoes Danced and Harps Played for Royalty	173
Captains, Arrangers and Managers	177
In the Stillness of the Night	179
Carnival Bungalow	181
Andre Garvey picks up where George and Arthur Coard left off	182
Mas' In Yu Mas'	185

Mas' Men 187
We Played Real Mas' 189
Diehard Supporters: No Pan Was Left Behind 197
Angel Harps Boycotted Mas' 200
IN 72 THE VIEUX COUR RECEICED A LICKING
WHAT WERE THEY THINKING? 201
Pictorial Interlude 206
Rupert Glean: None Came Close 250
What Carnival Come To? 253
First Dark-Skinned Carnival Queens 257
The Lime 261
Chinatown 267
Petrolina: The Girls, Can-Can, and Sailors 270
Prince Austin's First Visit to the Spice 273
The Spout 275
Inspector Hurley, James Lowe, and the Ganja Tree 278
Lord Melody - Punks 281
Mr. Redman 286
Uncle Paid Attention to His People: Emulations and
Recognitions 289
Rupert "Big Bear" Williams (Anthony DeRiggs) 292
Charlie Hood: Old Trafford and Carenage United 295
In Memorial: Dr. Winston Thomas 299
Panmen: In Memorial 301
He Keeps the Wharf Clean 308
Pictorial: The Sounds of Grenada in the Past 310
Broko on his instrument 318
Youthful Teasing and Taunting 319
Window-Shopping: Liking What We Could Not Afford 322
The Beauty of Christmas Eve 323
Christmas Eve Was Special 324
Christmas Then and Now 326
The Greasy (Ham) Pole 327
The Revolution: Hope and Betrayal of Trust 328
The Night 1500 Carroll Street Kitchen Closed 333

About the author 335

View of Cooper's Hill and the Wharf
(Photo credits: Anthony W. DeRiggs).

Aubrey "Paddy" DePradine: Cooper's Hill

MY FATHER, A man from Cooper's Hill, was a Wharf man and a quiet man who left us too soon. In the midst of my ambivalence, bewilderment, and confusion, his sickness and subsequent death triggered a subtle anger within me. I kept asking myself, "Why him?" He left us in his late forties, when children expected their fathers and mothers to be around to see and enjoy their grandchildren.

Aubrey, or "Paddy" as his friends and colleagues called him, was not a very tall man, unlike his brother Alphonso and his sister Mona. He was the fastidious type and loved his threads, which became more conspicuous when he was out of uniform. He was, like most of his companions back then, always groomed from head to toe. They carefully selected their felt hats to complement their Ban-Lon shirts and pleated trousers. Looking smart went beyond making a fashion statement; to them, it was a way of life.

My father made it a habit to always try on every new garment he bought—or came into possession of—to ensure he got the first wear out of the apparel. It was a ritual of his, which I have emulated to this day. Often, someone would ask him, "Didn't you just buy that?" I, too, have heard similar snipes, but who cares? It was his, and it was mine, and our reasons justified the purposes for our try-on. Most people who knew Paddy seldom saw him out of his khaki uniform, which he wore to work at the St. George's Pier as part of the water police. To this day, I am still baffled as to why they were called water police, considering they had no authority to apprehend or charge anyone on land or sea. Neither am I sure whether the title of water police existed back then as an official title in the public service.

Some who worked in that same capacity as my dad were "China Man" Salfarlie, nicknamed because of his slanted eyes; Mr. Ambrose, the inebriated one; Lenox "Laylay" James, father of soca artist Marcus "Lavaman" James; Dennis Phillip, a well-known panman and founding member of the Commancheros Steel Orchestra; and Mr. Briggs. One of the assignments given to my dad was that of venturing out into the inner harbor of St. George's to light the buoys. This was essential for guiding ships into port to be tethered to the pier. Today, with the advent of technology and the aid of well-equipped tugboats, that process is controlled much differently.

As young boys, we were always eager to accompany my dad on some of these choppy adventures in the small wooden watercraft that he maneuvered. This assignment had to be carried out in all types of weather (rain, sun, storms, or hurricanes). For us, fear was never a factor. We were in our preteens and relatively good swimmers, and riding the waves to reach the buoys became more of a charter than a challenge of fate. We were quite familiar with the seas, and swimming had become second nature to us. We spent a considerable amount of time in the seawater—nearly as much time as we spent on land. Swimming was a requirement to earn your badge as a Wharf Boy—whether diving for Miss Gutty's "Nigger Boy" (hard candy) or maneuvering tricks on the jetty for hours, which we did until our eyes resembled those of hind fish.

Friends of my dad often reminded us of his exceptional talent as a cricketer. They lauded him for his brilliant skills in his heyday and pointed to class prejudice as the reason he was never selected to play at a higher level of competition. The composition of the national cricket team consisted mainly of those from the affluent class. We were told that it was never his lack of competitiveness or competency; it was the community from which he came. As one of his close friends once lamented, "Paddy was a gifted cricketer, but he was also from the Wharf."

My dad and my uncle Gunny loved cricket and religiously followed the game (locally and internationally) on their transistor radios or the Philips radio at the house. A bit of irony was that their passion for cricket allowed them to admire the West Indian players, but they found it difficult to support West Indies as a team. Why? They felt the selectors were biased against players from small islands, such as Grenada, and that did not sit well with them. It therefore was justification enough to applaud the players but not Team West Indies. Gradually that resentment started to change when West Indies began the integration of small island players in their roster.

I knew fathers who "planassed" their children for the slightest infraction, but I honestly cannot remember a time when my father lifted his hand to chastise any of us. Remarkably, none of us suffered the scars of ill will or waywardness as a result. He left us in 1970, yet it still feels like yesterday. I became a man at the age of fifteen (during his illness) and a working man at the age of seventeen after his death. I was the eldest of all my brothers and one sister, and although he transcended in body, the values he left had a tremendous lifetime impact on me.

During his illness, I deliberately avoided going home because I was disgusted by the smell of Bengay ointment. Tirelessly, Bengay was employed by my grandmother and my aunt. They would rub it on his chest and back to bring him a measure of comfort, hoping his pain would subside. I immersed myself in the panyard (in the coal market) and rehearsed for the Steelband Festival, which was scheduled for December 1969. I did so even when the band was not in session. I simply did not feel any compulsion to climb that hill; the scent of Bengay reminded me of the efforts being made to halt the inevitable. We all had a difficult time facing the truth that my father was slowly slipping away to a place where we were not ready for him to go. Death was not in a hurry and waited patiently for the appropriate time to pay that untimely visit.

I recalled the glaze in his eyes as he sat on the Morris chair, staring toward Old Fort and the Catholic church. I was fast becoming wedged between a rock and the beginning of some hard places. His chest wheezed as he struggled to breathe with every inhalation; his weakened and wearied body was battered by this sickness in final preparation to meet his Maker. We were not prepared to welcome that thought. I kept asking myself, "Why him?" I could not fathom the thought of losing a father who was more of a friend to me. His stare, in sickness, left me helpless as a young boy and affected me for many years after his passing. I repeatedly asked, "Why him?"

I became angry and bitter, questioning whether God existed. Losing this quiet, genteel man did not make much sense to me. It was a difficult period for all of us—Chrissie (my mom), Tant Cho Cho (his mother), Uncle Gunny (his brother), and Tanty Mona (his sister)—as we watched him gradually slipping away. We all knew he was going, but surrendering before that final call was never an option. Fragile in appearance, he sank deeper and deeper into his own thoughts until the Lord bid him to come home. His death was the hardest place I encountered, and it took more than fifteen years to overcome.

Wharf, path leading to St. George's pier.

Inner harbor, St. George's.

Cooper's Hill, old and new.

Artist depiction of my dad, Aubrey "Paddy" DePradine.

My uncle, Alphonso "Gunny" DePradine.
Below: Aunty Mona and my mom, Chrissie.

Tant Cho Cho

MY GRANDMOTHER MARY DePradine (known to me as Tant Cho Cho) did not graduate from any medical institution as a nurse or a doctor, but there wasn't a sickness for which she did not have a remedy or cure. People from all strata of society (vendors, stevedores, schoolchildren, and parents of infants) sought her advice and care. Whether it was ear infection, colic, constipation, stoppage of water, tonsils, tapeworms, or asthma, Tant Cho Cho had a remedy for all—and amazingly yielded results. I occasionally invoke some of her remedies and cures when I lose trust in the contemporary directives given by the learned ones.

Tant Cho Cho was rigid in her food preparation and quite predictable with her ingredients. She always cooked rice with coconut cream, and I suspect that was the reason why the bun bun (rice stuck to the bottom of the pot, which required a bit of scraping) tasted so good.

She could never get our names correct when calling on us to "make a message" (a Grenadian phrase for running an errand to the shop to purchase or to credit or "truss" an item). My name varied from "Roy" to "You" to "You Boy." She once called on Shamrock (a young man living with Ms. Pearl, a cousin/neighbor) and, unable to remember his name, came up with "Rock and Roll" and "Rocky" (long before the movie starring Sylvester Stallone). To her, they were all one and the same. And that was Tant Cho Cho.

The Hill and the Standpipe: Where More than Water Flowed

THE STANDPIPE IN the middle of Cooper's Hill served the entire community, including the Cocoa. It was where our parents' washed clothes, engaged in gossip, and "throw words." It was the place where we took our George Otways (quick washing of feet and faces), a must before entering the house at night. The standpipe was a refreshing pit stop for those hurriedly beating the cobblestones to get to Empire Cinema to see a movie or hastily trying to get to work.

Back then, water was free, and the only time we (on the hill) saw someone from Water Commission (Bruno, Mr. Tamar, or Mr. Wiley) was not to collect arrears but to fix a busted pipe. Children were not allowed to gather around big people (adults) when they were engaged in conversations. We had to know our place. If curiosity or "fastness" propelled us too close to a conversation, very often someone would ask, "You lose something? Hurry up and find it." Such were the interactions by the standpipe on Cooper's Hill.

Cooper's Hill had three famous landmarks: the standpipe and two resident mango trees. The tree at the bottom of the hill was simply called "Terisita Mango" because it was in her yard. The other well-known mango tree was located at the middle of the hill in the yard of Cynthie (Cynthia Raymond). That mango tree was known as "Thick Skin," a fitting name for a fruit and representative of the type of bond, tightness, togetherness, and resoluteness that made Cooper Hill people exceptional as a community.

Ms. Terisita was the type of lady who did not waste her smile; not much amused her, and you had to be careful how you approached her, how you looked at her, what you uttered to her, and what you said about her "Uncle Gairy" (Sir Eric Gairy was Grenada's former prime minister). As boys, we said, "If Ms. Terisita was a judge, every accused coming before her would receive a life sentence." It was not until later that we realized she had more bark than bite.

Junior "Tatoes" (the Visigoth), as others referred to him, was the son of Ms. Terisita. Her tight grip on him may have restricted him from gallivanting and stifled his creativity as a young boy, but it didn't affect his craftiness in outsmarting her to his advantage when desired. In our unenlightened youthfulness, we came up with pejoratives for him (unfairly so), which exposed more of our ignorance than his inabilities.

Photo credit: Anthony W. DeRiggs. Chatting with his old friend Junior.

Junior (Tatoes/ The Visigoth) – Photos credit: Anthony Wendell De Riggs

Old Standpipe – Cooper's Hill

As children, the cobblestone high-rise that is Cooper's Hill was a piece of cake for us to maneuver (four, five, six times a day effortlessly). Today, it is our Kilimanjaro. I placed it on my bucket list, and whenever I return to Grenada, I climb that hill to satisfy my curiosity and measure what shape I am in. I attempted a few times I visited—from the bottom of the hill—but I only made it to the old standpipe. It wasn't because of exhaustion—though that played a part—or laziness. It was age. The spirit was excited, but the legs were hesitant to move. I concluded that a compromise must be reached to accomplish my task; the next try would begin from the top of the hill and end where I had abandoned my earlier attempts, by that same standpipe.

I felt a measure of sadness and emptiness after looking around and not hearing the voices I heard as a youth and the families who once occupied homes adjacent to that beautiful, lively cobblestone hill. Many left because of migration or destiny through death, which is the inevitable route that awaits us all. The cobblestones seemed unpolished and unrecognizable in their settings. Stones were once trampled on by the feet of many passersby and residents of the tightly knitted homes. The braggadocious spirit Cooper's Hill's people were known for was now silent. Between the residence of the Moore's house and the guides' hut—where we flew our kites during the Easter season and played games—is now an unkept, abandoned wilderness of shrubbery, begging for someone's attention.

View of the Wharf.

Present state of the Guides' Hut.

The stories, tales, and events of Cooper's Hill are no longer passed on except by a few: the likes of Anthony Wendell DeRiggs and Lincoln "Toro" DePradine in their publications; authors whose writings record the satisfaction experienced with Ms. Georgiana's and Ma Rubes's tamarind balls and sugar cakes, as well as Ms. Gutty's "Nigger Boy" candy, and Ms. Green's Conkies and Dada Ice Cream.

There are the tales of Old Man Ogias, also known as "Doctor," even if he had no medical degree. Doctor, according to local Grenadian folklore, encountered a "La Diablesse" by the rocks above the fire station area. However, Doctor isn't the only legendary figure. We can relate tales about "Dealers" selling and buying souls; Dufaye jumping through a window to escape "Duppy" while reading bad books; and Pitchet blowing his bugle every morning. Neighborhood folks claimed that the bugle blowing was Pitchet's signal to the "Ligaroos" that it was time to abandon flight.

All now in silence, and "all dat gone." Today's Cooper's Hill, by its silence, betrays what it was in time past. The names of Chrissie, Cho Cho, Pearl, "Big Gun," Cynthie, Tora, Terisita, Georgina, Gertude, Milina, Coslyn, Judith, Ogias, Leon, Evelyn, and Mary are uttered no more—and remembered only in time of reflections.

Ms. Georgina, Ma Rubes, and the tamarind (tambrand) balls.

Ms. Gertrude's coconut tart.

"Thick-skin" mango tree on Cooper's Hill.

The Steps

AS CHILDREN, WE sat on the steps, listened to "Nancy stories," and believed all tales had "happily-ever-after" endings. Our hopes were bundled in naive packages, influenced by what we saw in the movie houses and on movie screens. "Star Boy" always came out the winner, and that inspired us never to be crooks. The steps served as concrete wickets for the impromptu games we held as boys, competing under the bright lights of the lamppost in front of the house at the middle of the hill.

We fashioned empty Clorox bottles for balls. Fielding occupied every cobblestone on the hill, and the old standpipe was the boundary line to determine fours and sixes. We listened to test matches and became familiar with names such as Lance Gibbs, Rohan Kanhai, Clyde Walcott, Frank Worrell, Gary Sobers, Dennis Lillee, Sonny Ramadhin, Gordon Greenidge, Peter May, and Deryck Murray. We guessed the names of singers and songs played during WIBS request programs and lit candles on All Saints' Night for the departed.

We heard planes passing by in the sky and wondered if the time would ever come when we would be able to fly in those iron birds to the distant places we heard of, saw on screens, and identified on our school atlas. Such places included America, Canada, and Europe. We were keenly aware that those traveling to England did so by boat (the England Boat). From the steps, we saw them gathering on the Carenage with their grips, parasols, and hopes. A home is now constructed on that spot, but the steps remain. The new entrance is a reminder of the past.

The Hill, the People, and Their Politics

COOPER'S HILL WAS a very unique place with its hillside beauty and the panoramic view it afforded of the Carenage—from one end to the next. Perched on Cooper's Hill, we were privileged spectators of the inner harbor. We saw "cocoa boats" (lighters) and schooners off-loading, fishing boats, merchant ships such as *Starlight V*, and people interacting with "traffickers" to get their crates of produce and provisions to Trinidad and other destinations.

Cooper's Hill was unique in beauty and in unanimity too. Its residents were related as families. If not related by blood, it was by encroachment or by adoption. There were a few exceptions, such as the Medfords who lived at the top of the hill and the Lenore and Williams families. Most residing on Cobblestone Hill were staunch *Gairyites*—followers of Sir Eric Matthew Gairy—and none more so than my uncle Alphonso (Gunny) and Ms. Terisita who lived at the bottom of the hill. Their loyalty to Eric Gairy and his Grenada United Labour Party (GULP) was unwavering and uncompromising. They saw Gairy as a fighter for the poor, the common man, and the ordinary laborer on the streets, deprived and exploited by the plantocracy.

Later in life, I understood why those Gairyites, my uncle included, remained so adamant and dedicated in their support of Gairy. It had nothing to do with what they received from him; it had everything to do with what he promised to bring about for people like them. In 2004, Cooper's Hill was not spared the fury of Hurricane Ivan. It suffered the fate of many parts of Grenada. Homes on the beautiful hillside were battered, and debris was scattered, leaving remnants of the community that already had been suffering from depleted residency through internal and external factors, migration, and the sting of death. My father, uncle, aunt, grandfather, and cousins Eric "Malutt" Depradine and Reginald "Punchie" Fraser.

Youthful Eric Matthew.   Sir Eric Matthew Gairy.
Below: Eric Gairy (1950) delivering "adult suffrage" petition to the governor.

Eric Matthew Gairy: The Man, His Mystique, and His Mission

WILLIAM HUNDERT SAID, "Great ambition and conquest without contribution is without significance. What will your contribution be? How will history remember you?" History may remember Sir Eric Matthew Gairy, the Father of Independence, for many things: his rise, his downfall, his preoccupation with extraterrestrial life, and his aesthetics.

As time passes and the tone of conversations is no longer muffled by emotion and marked by sobriety, temperance, and honesty—not bias and malice—the contributions of this man must be weighed on a scale of fairness to assess his legacy. Some in their senior years may still find it a bit difficult to budge or let go of their deep-seated hatred. How significant is it that after these many years, the name of Eric Matthew Gairy still stirs such mixed emotions? Surprisingly, there seems to be an easement and a sense that the ripples of the past are gradually shifting to what he has accomplished (positively) rather than what he did negatively. The symbols he left are now absolving him of the sins he is accused of committing. Monuments and institutions that now are benefits to Grenada cannot be ignored. They have become an integral part of Grenadian life, and they serve as necessary buffers in the day-to-day commercial and economic traffic of today's Grenada. There are the construction of roundabouts and the green light to construct a medical school on our soil. Outside of his recognition as a visionary, it is an undeniable fact that Eric Matthew Gairy was an ingenious soul while he was the overseer of this nation.

Sir Eric Matthew Gairy: Parade awaiting his inspection and in his usual dapper mood

Side view of Cooper's Hill Today Photo compliments Anthony W. DeRiggs

Ogilvie House and the Big Stones: A Mystery Never Solved

IT BEGAN IN the early seventies, a few years after the Ogilvies moved into their home at the bottom of Cooper's Hill. Prior to their occupation, the homes adjacent to Marryshow Pasture and the residents of Cooper's Hill and its surrounding areas had access to a walkway they took advantage of to peruse the community. Indicative of many of his socioeconomic status, Ogilvie constructed a fence to block the shortcut. The fencing ran up the side of his property to an area a few feet from the standpipe. This was not something we were accustomed to in that community, and many of our families and neighbors did not take that lightly. Ogilvie said the fencing was to protect his fruit trees, but, to us, it was a statement of the elite separating themselves from the rest.

Stones started raining on Ogilvie's house. The first barrage of stones drew the attention of the police, and many suspects were confronted. The first was a fella we called "Poor B." He lived a stone's throw (no pun intended) across from the Ogilvie's constructed fence, close to Marryshow Pasture. That investigation did not bear any fruits. The second suspect was Norris "Fox" Stevens, and that inquiry also fell flat.

As the stones continued to pound Ogilvie's roof—unabated and with impunity—Ogilvie turned his attention to Frankie Raymond. Frankie was nothing close to an acolyte or a choirboy; he had a very mischievous side to him. Frankie lived just above the boundary fence with his mom, Cynthia. She was a police officer, but that did not bring solace to the accuser or impede the police from conducting their investigation.

As the police were in the process of interrogating Frankie, the stones began to sink on the roof of the house with ferocity and vengeance. This was enough for the police to conclude that neither Poor B, Fox, nor Frankie had anything to do with that strange episode. It became so frequent, expected, and without warning that area residents did not flinch or even take cover during these episodes.

Another strange phenomenon had to do with the size of the stones that were retrieved from the rooftop. The size did not match the sounds they produced. We asked, "How could what sounded like rocks and boulders be no bigger than pebbles?"

Ogilvie's daughter Susan often sat on their veranda when the deluge of rocks began flooding the rooftop. She would only shrug her shoulders and smile. The community residents and passersby alike became used to the falling stones, not flinching or being afraid of being struck by one of the mysterious projectiles. To this day, no one can explain with certainty who, what, or where these missiles came from. We had our suspicions, though many would dismiss them as being overly dramatic—and us of being too superstitious. This mysterious drama only ended when the family migrated to Canada.

The Ogilvie house (on the right).

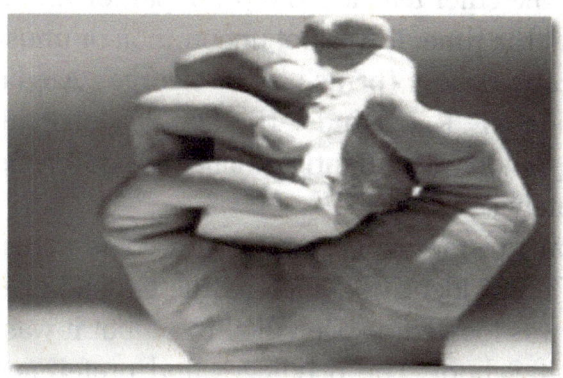

School, Community, and Class

MANY OF THE residents of Cooper's Hill and surrounding areas were members of the Anglican faith, through ceremonial baptism and confirmation, apart from a sprinkling of Catholics, Methodists, and Seventh-day Adventists. As baptized and confirmed Anglican Church members, the expectation and the school selected to attend were never in doubt; at times, some parents opted for the Methodist or Wesley Hall School, also called the Morris School, because of the prompting of an influential family member. Most, if not all, of the DePradine and Fraser clan, and the Thomas families from the Cocoa and the Wharf, attended the Anglican school on Church Street.

Back then, church affiliation was the determining factor for which school you attended. Many of these institutions were known by the chief teacher, the principal, or the headmaster in charge at the time. It was not uncommon or unusual to hear of Mr. Jacob's School (principal St. George's Anglican Senior School, prior to E. R. L. Hinds), Hindsey School, Palmer School, or Morris School. Ms. Baptiste School and Teacher Blanche were privately run.

Only on rare occasions would you come across a school with a different identifier, such as the Grenada Government School. It was located on Melville Street, but it was called the Back Street School. The privileges and preferences of class filtered into the school system and played a very significant role in determining the destiny of some students in unbelievably subtle and clandestine ways, which had lasting negative effects.

As Wharf Boys, we experienced the unfairness and its residue, but some may say that it is just our perception. We experienced firsthand what was practiced in the system. Quite often, we felt as if we were rowing against the tide by not being given a fair deal as it pertained to class-assigned promotions. After leaving the junior school setting (standard 3), students were promoted to the senior school at the upstairs level, beginning with standard 4. This transition signaled the trajectory of your academic future. The assignment of the standard 4—A or B—determined whether you were destined for scholarship class or the doors.

The 4-Bs were highways to scholarship class in standard 5; 4A and 4D prepared you for the workforce. We were all aware of this, but it never dampened our thirst for learning and performing at our best. What energized this perception? We noted academics versus acquaintances; who knew who and which family name carried weight. We, sitting in classrooms with others, knew their academic capabilities; when preferential treatment was given, it wasn't a stretch for us to conclude why. It was tendered to them because of accessibility.

We were not the only ones singled out for separation based on where we came from (the Wharf). Communities such as River Road, the Point, Lower Springs, and Belmont did not fare any better; for some reason, the Wharf carried a stigma like no other. I struggle to understand what sin we Wharf boys had committed to deserve such treatment.

E. R. L. Hinds was our headmaster during my sojourn at Hindsey School. He was slim and about five foot nine. Like most families from Mount Moritz, he easily could have passed as a Caucasian because of his complexion. To his credit, he was a brilliant orator, and he was very knowledgeable on current issues of international affairs. Each morning, after prayers at general assembly, we bellowed out a couple English or Scottish folklore songs, and then he provided updates on world issues before dismissal to our various classrooms.

Without any concrete evidence—just based on intuition and reasonable suspicion—we felt that Mr. Hinds exhibited some prejudicial tendencies toward us and other stigmatized communities. Our intuitiveness and suspicion were reinforced based on statements Mr. Hinds occasionally would utter indirectly. We became sensitive to them. He was a disciplinarian, and he exerted all his strength through his thick leather strap—while biting the end of a matchstick he held on the side of his mouth for reinforcement. We expected brute force whenever we observed him rolling up his shirt sleeves his elbows and stroking his blond hair to the side. It was a sure indication that "Masa force" was on its way.

For us, being diverted from 4-B was never because we lacked the academic accruements. Our competencies were supported by our junior school report cards. Having said that, I must confess that we were never eager to be on the plantation of Mr. Hinds, given his propensity to use undue force on us with his leather weapon and the disdain we suspected he had for us as Wharf boys.

Class and color came before competencies. These criteria, of course, prevented many of us from making it into that exclusive club. I know am not hallucinating; this perception was, and still is, unanimous among my peers. Nevertheless, we had the good fortune of encountering a few competent, fair-minded teachers (male and female) on our journeys.

Ms. Irva Baptiste taught in 4-B, but very few of us had the good fortune of being in her class. With Ms. Baptiste, one was able to see an attempt to move away from the sifting process—from the separation of the goats from the sheep and the lessening of the influences of those in society who had a voice to speak and a determined push to assist those who were considered weak. Outside of her career as a teacher, Ms. Baptiste is credited for penning the Grenada National Anthem. Always immaculately dressed and slender, she "repped" her high heels as a stately, sophisticated socialite.

Andre Adams, a standard 4 teacher, marred his abilities to be an exceptional tutor as he misdirected his energies on trying to impress the young ladies in the class rather than focusing on the curriculum set before him. Mr. Sealy was considered a product of the Wharf, but he showed no partiality to those he knew or those who were related to him (the Thomas family). His whip knew no boundary and came with equal force. However, his Friday-afternoon classes on Greek mythology were captivating and interesting.

Two teachers who made a great impression on us were Mr. Ottley and Mr. Basil Horford (may his soul rest in peace). Both recognized our abilities as students and encouraged us with a balance of worth, acceptance, and insight—not based on where we came from but on what we were capable of doing.

Elbert. R. L. Hinds (Hindsey).

Irva Baptiste

Basil Harford.

Mr. Sealy (right) looking on intensely at a class on a school outing.

Once we got to the fourth standard, it was either the 4-H Club or the "Technical Wing," a skills-training school for tradesmen located at the entrance of Tanteen. The school was our preference because of the latitude and liberty it afforded us for truancy or, as we called it, to "skull." We took full advantage to "skull."

Very rarely did Mr. Roberts, the principal of the Technical Wing, see us for our scheduled Monday class. Mr. Roberts was a tall, robust man with a no-nonsense attitude. At times, he had the audacity of raising his hands with a strap to correct us if we failed to draw a straight line with our rulers. His behavior was added incentive for us to "skull" and find a more pleasurable way of occupying our Monday mornings.

The home of Winston (Maga) became our alternate place of assembly. We cooked whatever was available and sipped on Mr. Barr's Black and White scotch whiskey, which he kept hidden in the house. At other times, we ended up at the residence of the Checkley family, and Brian Checkley served as the ringleader. That house was a stone's throw away from that of the Steele residence, which is where Rawle lived.

On a particular Monday morning of "skulling", Brian invited us to visit his home to do the cooking. After searching the kitchen, the only ingredients available were a small brown bag of rice and a box of custard. Brian decided he would experiment with both (strange combination). In preparing the meal, Brian mistakenly poured kerosene into the pot instead of oil; it was white rice and mustard sautéed with kerosene. What a mixture! We all decided it was too risky to eat from that pot, but Brian insisted otherwise. He threatened if we did not eat his food, he will have no choice but to expose us by calling out to Ms. Elma (Rawle's mom) who was just a clothesline away, to tell her where he was. Fearing exposure, we reluctantly obliged to eat that curious combo; weeks later our belches felt like leaking gas stations.

To further our tribulations and add to our troubles, at the end of that year, Mr. Hind's request the boys attending the Technical Wing to bring all our completed crafted woodwork to the school for an exhibition. The request caught us all by surprise. We hurriedly tried to come up with something—any kind of woodwork—to satisfy Mr. Hind's request. Rawle was skillful with his hands, and he had no problem constructing a beautiful jewelry box. He also helped the rest of us hastily fashion quick fixes such as washing or "jooking" boards, wooden spoons, and swizzle sticks to meet the exhibition deadline. I do not know how, but we pulled it off. Miraculously!

Side view of Hindsey School yard.

Introduction to the Wharf Community

AS IF TIRED of hearing my constant propping up of the Wharf, someone said to me, "Do you know there is more to Grenada than the Wharf?" I understood why that question was uttered, and I had no problem with it. I replied, "You pick your place, and I will pick my space." Today, the Wharf is not known as the place where many great "Mas" bands paraded. It's now the place where "Dirty" mas trample and string lights and advertisements are wrapped around revelers as aprons during Monday Night Mas.

I reminisce of the Wharf of artistry, of great masquerade creators and creations, and of cultural icons who excelled and succeeded in everything from pan to Mas pageantry and stage shows that are yet to be matched by others. No one can forget the likes of Daisy Commisiong, George Coard, "Away" Lindsay, Ken Sylvester, Richardo "Ricky" Keens-Douglas, Tan Tan, Willie B, Ming, and Andre Garvey of Garvey and Associates. Some may take issue with the list of names mentioned, but the Carenage is different from the Wharf.

The Carenage is the umbrella curve; the Wharf is the tarpaulin spread of communities extending to Green Street, Tyrrel Street (Herbert Blaize Street), Park Lane, Cooper's Hill, Goat Hill, and a section of Tanteen by family association, but it was even more than just a geographic location. Though often stigmatized, it produced many educators, poets, and sportsmen and women. It housed factories, restaurants, and the main entry seaport (piers and docks) and was the major goods distribution point for the entire country.

It was a bustling center of activities, a "mecca of commerce," and a community of families—many related by friendship and not blood. It is not difficult to explain why those of us from that community are so passionate about a place. So many of us were marginalized, ostracized, and stigmatized, and we were never credited with positives or the accomplishments and contributions of community residents.

The famous Whitsuntide Games were one of the most highly regarded and respected events in the region in the 1960s. This prestigious meet brought to the shores of Grenada the best of the best in competition. The competitors included Roger Gibbons (the renowned Trinidad and Tobago cyclist), Hasley Crawford (another Trinidadian who won the Olympic hundred-meter gold medal in 1976 in Montreal), Donald Pierre, Raymond Roberts, Roger Byer, Raymond Anthony, the Friday brothers, and Joe "B" Brown from Tanteen. This marquee "mini olympic," Whitsuntide, was organized, subsidized, and carried out by a club from the Wharf Sporting Club, which also produced some of the best footballers in Grenada at that time.

Members of Sporting Club.

Executive members of the Sporting Club (MEP Publishers)

Photo above: Compliments: MEP Publishers...Photo right: Compliments Right: Roger: Left to Right: Cleo Peters, Roger Byer, and Ian "Psycho" St. Bernard.

Raymond Roberts (distance runner), Donald Pierre (distance runner), and P. C. Gibbs. The 1972 Grenada Athletic squad (Fitzgerald "Naka" Joseph).

Hasley Crawford, 1976 Olympic gold medalist (Trinidad and Tobago).

Joe "B" Brown from Tanteen (cyclist).

Like most other communities, the Wharf was a mixed bag of the good, the bad, and the ugly. In many ways, the successes were often ignored by others; instead, recipients received more negative accusations than accolades.

Much more than a picturesque curve, the Wharf also was a bustling commercial and entertainment district that was responsible for many talented panmen. In 1965, three of them came together to form Angel Harps, which is Grenada's oldest steel orchestra. The commercial outfits included the Empire Theatre, factories (cigarettes, soft drinks, ice cream, and ice), supermarkets, bakeries, laundry-marts; and restaurants. Port St. George accommodated military ships, cruise liners, and cargo boats.

Indeed, it was a vibrant community of commerce with talented individuals in academics, sports, and culture. The community's greatness—and the opportunities to participate in sports and culture—prepared us to face the inevitable challenges of life. Tanteen, the Pan House in the "Coals Market," the swimming and fishing on the Princess Margaret Jetty, and other activities served as a bond of togetherness. With ease, we effortlessly stroked our way from the jetty to the other side of the Carenage and back to the jetty. We did it just for the fun of it! When tempted, we would swim to Mount Pandy and then continue to the beginning of Grand Anse Beach.

For a time, our adventure shifted from the jetty to the raft. That raft was anchored in the Carenage waters. It was placed there by the Henry family; they owned the ice factory where the Grenada Postal Corporation is now located. Before school and on Sundays, someone would shout, "Boys, for the raft!" And then the splashing would last for hours.

Clevroy "Depo" DePradine

Swimming to the raft

Things That Existed on the Wharf/Carenage at One Time or Another

- The Lime Factory
- ice factory
- cigarette factory
- bakeries
- laundry mart/dry cleaning (Martinizing)
- sweet drink factory (Stroudies)
- Pebbles (Ice Cream)
- fire station
- Empire Cinema
- telephone company
- cable and wireless (telegraph)
- Nutmeg Restaurant
- Chinatown
- Cold Storage (supermarket)
- Rock N Roll (Supermarket and Chinese restaurant)
- post office
- Cubby Hole (nightclub)
- shops (Harbin, "Brofit," Nedd, Commansing, Rush, LH, Miss Baby)
- Bobby's/Kyam's (tire stores)
- Gittens Pharmacy

The Wharf: A Tourist Delight

BEFORE THE CONSTRUCTION of the Esplanade Mall and Cruise Ship Port on Melville Street, tourist liners berthed the St. George's Pier or anchored in the inner harbor. We welcomed the likes of the *Argonaut, Stella Solaris, Odyssey, Carnival Liners,* the *QE II,* and many others. This gave an opportunity to steelbands such as Angel Harps, Panasonic, and South Stars to make a change by performing aboard the cruise liners.

Invariably, the visitors, stepping onto the port, were greeted by a contingent from a local folklore group, which was accompanied by the sound of steel. The scenery of Grenada, from both sea and by land, was a tourist's delight. Some visitors patronized Joe Pitt's Souvenir Gift Shop, purchasing arts and crafts made by Grenadians. Others chose taxi excursions to explore the island. The vast majority of visitors opted to walk the curve around the Wharf, a fitting introduction and invitation to the beautiful Isle of Spice.

The French architectural buildings dotting the landscape were a prime attraction. The Anglican, Presbyterian, and Catholic churches served as a "halo of approval" to this remarkable beauty. It was a captivating sight to behold. The slow walk around the Carenage—a postcard experience with captivating scenery—afforded local tourist vendors the chance to ply their goods, to their satisfaction, at a reduced bargained price. This is what a writer for a prestigious travel magazine said about the Carenage: "It may not be Willemstad, but as picturesque Caribbean ports go, the Carenage is supremely captivating"

Postcard photos

Kenrick "Malutt" DePradine (under the rod). *Brighter Out of Darkness* tenor trio: Clevroy "Depo" DePradine, Martin "Rabbit" Church, and Cosley Boyke playing on a tourist boat gig.

MS *Argonaut*.

Bianca C: The Wharf to the Rescue

AS A PEOPLE, it is not difficult to identify the things that annoy Grenadians the most; we cannot hide these annoyances. The politicians would know, the pastor will hear, and the priest will not have to guess when we are annoyed. Outside of that, Grenadians are a welcoming people; when there is a need, "tabey" is suspended to do what is necessary for goodwill to prevail and manifest itself. Without question, we will step up to the plate—even if we must complain later.

The "Christ Statue," located on the Carenage/Wharf, is a testament and reminder of our goodwill, our virtue of selflessness, which we are capable of demonstrating at times. On October 22, 1961, *Bianca C,* a luxury cruise ship caught fire in the outer harbor of St. George's. Without hesitation, our people on land readied themselves to assist, and those at sea approached the smoking ship without knowing what to expect or what danger awaited them.

Fishermen on the Wharf hastily freed their vessels to reach the engulfed liner. Every floater on the island, including rowboats and fishing boats, was utilized in rescuing the crew and passengers. Stevedores and water police—like my dad—were called into action. We were used to infernos on land, but a cruise ship on fire was not an accustomed site. Courtney "Grubay" Renwick, known for his expertise in the water, played a valiant roll in the rescue mission. He was a customs officer on St. George's Pier the time of the incident.

Without the selfless efforts of Grenadians that day, the fatalities may have well exceeded the one individual who lost his life in the inferno. The GBSS Tanteen Barracks was quickly transformed into makeshift shelters for the distressed passengers. Grenada's Red Cross, Boy Scouts, Girl Scouts, and Cadets—along with civilian volunteers—formed brigades to assist. The Italian government later donated a statue, "Lady of the Sea," to Grenada in recognition of their kindness on that October day in 1961.

The wreckage of *Bianca C* is one of the most famous scuba diving treats in the world.

University of Empire: An Institution Called Angel Harps

EMPIRE CINEMA AND the surroundings amenities, including hardware and food stores, and Angel Harps Steel Orchestra, served the Wharf community well. Empire was more than a cinema; it was an institution of higher learning (Empire University).

Many great performers—including calypsonians and soul groups such as the Meters—graced the stage of this prestigious institution. As carnival season approached, the covered lobby of Empire Cinema became a courtyard. Masqueraders and spectators eagerly awaited the commencement of the big show. It was our place to congregate, and every step was a pulpit. On the Empire's steps, one had to be prepared to take "take tone" (old talk, as we said back then). Any misstep or mistake could become a yoke around your neck for life or an alias that would follow you to the grave.

The steps to the front gate also served as beds for the tired to recuperate and the weak to regain their strength. The steps gave those who were inebriated a place to rest their heads without interference. Under the shaded area of the lobby, masqueraders would gather to await—with a sense of pride and great anticipation—the other members of their carnival band section. Everyone listening to Angel Harps warming up the atmosphere. It was a signal to get ready and get dressed.

Sadly, Empire Cinema was demolished and there is the Spice Isle Imaging health clinic (a vexing contrast). Empire—this institution of higher learning, this university, this place of refuge, this iconic structure—is but a memory. The neon lights of Empire that once cascaded across the water have disappeared, the "limers" and vagabonds are gone, and Ms. Baby's shop is closed permanently.

Empire Cinema and a view of the Cocoa.

From the Cinema Screen to the CID

MAS BAND portrayal: "TO HELL AND BACK"

IN THE LATE 1950s, the police chief of pre-independent Grenada was a white South African by the name of Holly. For many years, we had assumed that Holly was an Englishman because of the colonial attachments, obligations, and stranglehold the

British had on us—from estates to plantations, courts of law, and Parliament. Our assumption was also informed by the English connection to our churches and schools, the Royal Grenada Police Force (RGPF), and the Richmond Hill Prison, which was named after Her Majesty Queen Elizabeth. Every institution was under the subjection of the queen's dictate.

After learning that he was South African, we were able to put many things into perspective, including his attitude and temperament. He was a tall, lanky man, and he ran the police force with a sturdy hand. Grenada did not have an army contingent outside of the police force, but Holly commandeered his officers like a regiment of highly trained soldiers. His sternest was not lost on his narrow "massa" features.

In the fifties, there was a carnival war Mas band named "To Hell and Back," prompted, I am sure, by the World War II flick starring Audie Murphy. A similar portrayal was displayed during the carnival period the previous year in Trinidad and Tobago.

To Hell and Back was brought to the streets of St. George's, and Holly, to ensure peace, fixed his keen eyes on the masqueraders, especially the young men from the Green Street area. He noticed the agility and seriousness of a few in the MP section of the band as they crossed the stage in Queens Park. Holly was deeply impressed, and he decided these men could be an asset to him as members of the RGPF. He proceeded to enlist them in the Royal Grenada Police Force. No theoretical exams were needed or administered to the new police recruits, and physical dexterity was not necessary to prove fitness.

This was the mechanism—beginning with a Hollywood movie and then interpreted in a Mas band—through which the RGPF found some of its officers, elevating the Criminal Investigation Department to an elite department. Holly's recruits from To Hell and Back included "Boragee" Sylvester, Rex, and the Mitchell brothers from Green Street (the sons of the infamous Merry Mitchell).

In an ironic twist, the Mitchell Brothers of the CID elite squad became the nemesis of the Wharf Boys, monitoring their every move and action and being strict to the point of threatening arrest should anyone not abide by the law.

The last of the Mitchell brothers played cello pan for the original Angel Harps and was also a member of the Grenada Coast Guard before relocating to the United States.

The Wharf by Night

Long gone are the reflections of Empire,
No more neon lights at night, stretching across the tranquil waters.
The steam streaming from the Lime Factory?
Regrettably, that is all but a distant memory.
The eager feet of patrons anxious to catch a show,
People going to and fro.
The Wharf was once the center of commerce for sure.

This is now the Wharf by Night.
Dimmed today—but still bright with memories.
No longer do we see the ripples of sprats and long-gar fishes.

No more tempting smells or fragrant aromas of the nutmeg dishes.
The "Boueese" sounds from the cinema have ceased—
Since Empire Cinema became deceased,
The entertainment capital, the Wharf, seems now at ease—
except for the sounds of katydids, crickets, and the harbor breeze.
But we can still enjoy the wharf by night.
It will never be the place we once knew,
Yet treasured memories live—and not just a few.
Still, we can enjoy the wharf by night.

It Was Here on the Wharf

WELL, I SAY no more. "Mafu" shouted, "Boy, wen last?"

Pants Margaret asked a dockworker, "How you smiling so, the eagle mess or what?"

Old Man Polar Bear, with an engine on his back, sang "I did it my way" by Frank Sinatra.

On the Wharf, we heard Grubay and his stories. All of us knew he embellished his tall tales, but we never dared call them lies. It was a place where "mushing" left you stained but never disfigured. The bungalow had more traffic than Lagoon Road. Empire showed movies at 1:30 p.m., 4:30 p.m., and 8:30 p.m. Westerns starred Audie Murphy, Dan Duryea, and Jack Palance. Wang Yu and Bruce Lee made fighting look easy. Families were drawn to seeing *The Sound of Music*, starring Julie Andrews, Christopher Plummer, and the von Trapps of Austria.

We remember the Wharf when Angel Harps, with its panhouse in the Coals Market, practiced songs in a repertoire ranging from calypso to classic. The Brofitt Shop was bustling, and its proprietor, Brother B, would give you a six-month ban for dropping the F sharp in his shop.

The Lime Factory kept the aroma of lime in the air, and the Nutmeg Restaurant tempted us with the "chicken snack" smell whizzing along with the Wharf breeze.

The fire truck—known to the public as "Halter Back"—took two hours to travel from the fire station to the post office to put out a fire. The immigration office, which was immediately adjacent to the fire station, burnt to the ground before Halter Back and its crew could put out the fire.

The excitement of the community was augmented by characters such as Joe Pitt and politicians who were never elected.

A car went through Herbert's house, and they found him with the tip of the Phoenix cigarette still in his mouth. He whispered, "Why you all disturbing me?"

Joe Pitt drove his car into the sea and said he was only parking it.

Gairy transformed the Wharf into a white sandy beach.

Mas Bands gathered on the Wharf, and Herby made the masquerade of "Away Lindsay" famous. In a quiet voice, he would always whisper, "Mas Mas, play 'Away,' Mas."

It was also alleged that a certain Wharf man went to London, England, and came back because he forgot a five-dollar bill in a vase at his home in Grenada.

"Daddy Old Man."

Brofitt Shop and Marshall Shop

OF ALL THE places of business in the area, attention must be paid to two: Brofitt Shop and Marshall Shop. Marshall Shop was located at the bottom of Park Lane, adjacent to Tyrell Street (now Herbert Blaize Street), and Brofitt Shop was central on the Carenage.

The congregants at Marshall Shop were drawn by the "spirits" and not the Holy One. An eighth of rum was limited to one drinker, but a quart drew the interest of a few. The drinkers around Marshall Shop were never prone to any kind of violent outbursts—drunk or sober—but they had mastered cussing. Words and expressions laced with poetic venom made their conversations and exchanges unsuitable for the ears of children.

In its prime, this shop served those who depended on "trussing" (buying and paying later). Names were written in a registry that detailed purchases. Mr. Marshall also was a barber (we called him the executioner), and he preferred to use a hair clipper the size of a lawn mower instead of scissors. Many times, we would plead with him to save our muffs, and with deaf ears, he would plow through our pride spitefully or deliberately.

Brofitt Shop was of a different caliber. No alcohol was sold there. Brother Brathwaite was a preacher and a member of the Gospel Hall Church. Unlike Marshall Shop, there was no "trussing" at Brofitt Shop. He made that clear with a sign above the counter: "Don't ask for Mr. Credit. He is dead and buried. Mr. Bad Pay attended his funeral."

Brofitt sold the best pig snout and crispy fishcakes crunched in the middle of Vienna and leaven bread. "Snowball and milk" were a delight. Brother B dished out suspensions to those who misbehaved in his shop or used obscenities. He usually administered six-month bans for overbearing recklessness.

Sam Bristol (Ugly Sam) entered the shop, made suggestive gestures, and sang, "Jam totie, jam totie!"

Brother B shouted, "Sam, take six months!"

Brofitt and Marshall Shops.

Under Empire

AT EMPIRE, THE wearied sought refuge from the scorching heat as they mumbled to themselves. It was not because they were insane; it was to figure out whether it should be "back and neck" again for lunch or pig tail or salt fish. Salt fish was not what it is today with all those fancy names; it was just salt fish. For anything under a quarter pound, you asked for it softly.

The shopkeeper would shout, "Did you say salt fish?"

Under Empire, the "hardback" and the "hardheaded" congregated. It was a place where racquetball was played. Chinese Checkers was played for hours with Saccema, Nose, Maloney, and others. Under Empire, you heard whose child belongs to whom, who was horning whom, and who was owing whom. Debates on local politics and international issues—from the Vietnam War to the Pan African and Black Power Movements—that were sweeping the region.

Under Empire, Nella and Milena tactfully threw words and watched each other with crossed eyes. They knew who went in and who came out without keeping written notes. Under Empire, you could find Ulric anytime he was in Grenada. He would be sitting with a washrag on his head as a "Nowhere-ian."

Mas and Laugh

 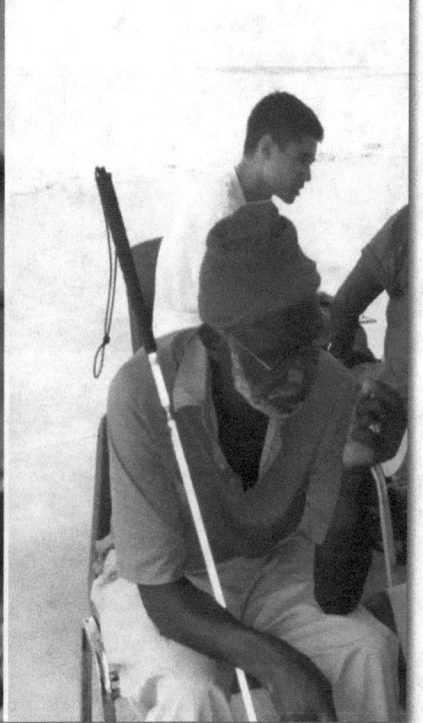

Lincoln "Ming" Andrews.   "Ming" Andrews in his senior years.

BY THE EMPIRE, Ming depicted "King George slaying the dragon." He boldly asked the adjudicators to judge him from the front and for photographers to take pictures only from the front. The back of the Ming's float was incomplete. Those standing under Empire Cinema understood Ming's dilemma and were in stitches to see him depicting King George only from the front.

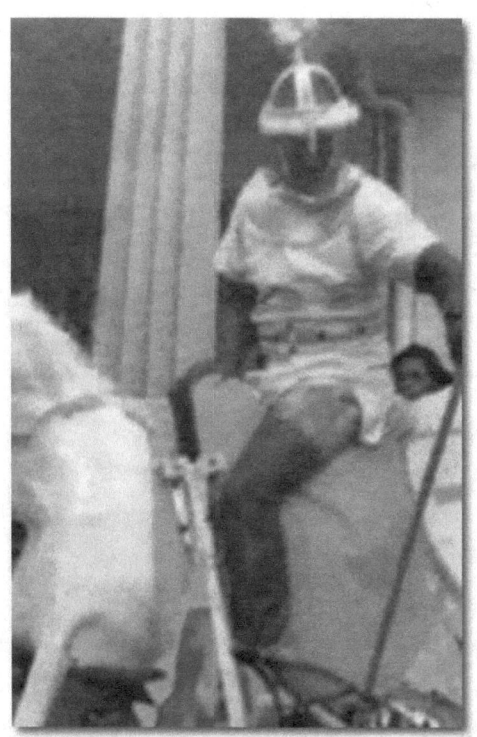
"Ming" Andrews as King George.

The Character and the Characters from the Wharf

Courtney "Grubay" Renwick: The Man and the Legend

GRUBAY, AS THE Wharf raconteur, was the best of the best. His satirical sense of humor was unmatched, and his tall tales gripped in every story he told. We had many similar to him, but there were none who matched him.

His suspenseful anecdotes, at times, left us wondering whether what we heard from Grubay took place; his was the track record of a bona fide fabulist. One tale was about a lady named Ms. Gaskin.

Ms. Gaskin, according to Grubay, owned the sweetest "Julie mango" tree in St. George's. He said the mangoes were so sweet that bees chose to have a "bee convention" on it every year. However, no one could get close to Ms. Gaskin's Julie mangoes because she had four bad dogs, and one guarded the north side of her fence. The other dogs guarded the south side, the east side, and the west side.

Every mango season, the guys from the Wharf and Green Street area tried to put their hands on a few of Ms. Gaskin's Julie mangoes. Grubay boasted, however, that he could deliver half the mangoes on the tree.

One evening, the boys challenged Grubay to do what they had been trying to accomplish for years. After Ms. Gaskin was asleep, Grubay went to Ms. Gaskin's house to fulfill his boastful claim.

The dogs began to bark as soon as Grubay crossed the fence, but he entered Ms. Gaskin's gate. The dogs were barking from the north, south, east, and west. Ms. Gaskin, knowing how protective and vicious her dogs were, did not poke her head outside her window to investigate.

Grubay opened the gate and slapped the first dog that came toward him. The slap was so hard that the other dogs pretended they were asleep. Another effect of the slap, Grubay said, was the Anglican church bell rang twice, making some people believe that communion was being served. That settled, Grubay proceeded to the mango tree.

He exited through the gate with the main branch of the mango tree. The method he employed, Grubay said, was ripping the tree in half and giving it one shake. The bounty of mangoes was shared with the neighborhood residents. Grubay reported that every house had one crocus bag full of Ms. Gaskin's Julie mangoes—and none was left on the main branch that he had taken from the tree.

Grubay wasn't yet finished. After the distribution of mangoes, he said he returned to Ms. Gaskin's yard and nailed the branch to the rest of the tree—without awaking Ms. Gaskin. The following mango season, to the surprise of Ms. Gaskin, half the tree was green—and the other half was dry. Ms. Gaskin went to her grave convinced that it was the work of a bad spirit; she thought somebody in the neighborhood had worked obeah on her.

Tall Tales or Lies

In the Caribbean, those of us who grew up in the time before iPhones, iPads, and the Internet found time for laughter. Our stress relievers did not come from smartphones. They came from smart, humorous people such as Courtney "Grubay" Renwick. Every so often, we reminisce by pulling out one of his tall tales from the troves of his treasure chest of laughter. We also securely guarded the memories of individuals who, through the art of storytelling, allowed us to differentiate "tall tales" from "lies." It is always important to make the distinction between a liar and one who tells tall tales. What is the difference? A liar consciously says things to deceive, but the one who tells tall tales leaves it up to you to believe or not.

Here is another of Courtney "Grubay" Renwick's classics. He was a stout man with the physical attributes and skills one expected from someone far less weighty than he was. The one thing all agreed on, without a doubt, was that Grubay—Miss Bernadine's son—was an exceptional swimmer.

His catalog of tall tales is too numerous to mention, but I will share one more. In this episode, it was Grubay's encounter at an "Ole Years Night Dance" at the St. Dominic's R.C. School in St. David.

Grubay said it was the best Ole Year's Night dance, second only to the one held at the St. James Hotel. The St. Dominic's R.C. dance attracted "Saga Boys" from all over St. George's, including the Wharf. Grubay said the girls from St. David's loved him for his acrobatics on his motorbike and for his looks. He was the only fella on the Wharf who mastered the technique of dancing Castilian with two to three women at a time. His friends had to beg—and sometimes were forced to pay him—in order to get a dance.

One particular night, Ole Year's night, the musicians playing at the school were from Crochu and the areas of St. David. They made the mistake of bringing their girlfriends to the party that night. Grubay said, from the time he entered the dance hall, the women went crazy—band members' girlfriends ("tout bagay – tout moon"). He said there was no rest for the wicked (pointing at himself).

After a while, Grubay sensed that something was awry. The bandsmen began playing in the wrong keys and getting angrier as their girlfriends literally fell all over Grubay. Then a fight broke out on the dance floor. Grubay, looking around, noticed there were no Wharf men in sight. He was alone in a big fight in the middle of the dance hall.

Clevroy "Depo" DePradine

The drummer of the band, Sambo, was a real "badjohn." Grubay was not a liar; he just told tall tales. After beating up the band members and leaving them bruised, Grubay told us he went home to the Carenage. He left the brawl and the battered men with not a scratch on his body or a blemish on his suit. He had no idea where Filo and the other Carenage fellas disappeared to after the fight started.

After taking a bath and hanging up his suit in the living room, Grubay said he heard a faint voice whispering, "Help! Help"! Grubay searched the entire house and saw no one. He went back to bed, and the cry began again. He went outside and saw no one. Grubay decided to check his suit. He looked in his jacket pocket, and found Sambo, the drummer, coiled up with his drumstick in his hand.

We asked, "How come your jacket pocket did not rip?"

Grubay paused, broke into his signature thunderous laugh, and then stated, "Good gabardine, man. Good gabardine."

Grubay was not a liar; he only told tall tales.

The Day Grubay Became Easter Water Parade MC

UNCLE GAIRY LEFT his footprints from marine sports for us to emulate, but we are yet to see or accomplish anything close to what he brought to the Wharf and the shores of Grenada when he conceptualized the idea of an Easter Water Parade. The annual event was implemented with precision and was flawlessly executed. Though many saw it as a risk, it was a risk that Uncle was willing to take.

The event gained the respect of even those who had publicly ridiculed the man. They became fans of his spectacular water festival, which is now synonymous with Uncle Gairy and deservedly so. The Easter Water Parade was different, and it was memorable. The Carenage was transformed into a man-made white sandy beach with boat races, swimming, greasy poles, and water polo contests.

The selection of Courtney "Grubay" Renwick as Easter Water Parade MC brought a considerable amount of flair to the activities. He employed colorful words to admonish the stubborn when his instructions were not followed. We all thought putting a mic in the hands of Grubay with his unpredictable, unabashed way with words, was a horrendous mistake—and we were correct.

Between my Rock & some Hard Places

Former home of Courtney "Grubay" Renwick (Darryl Brathwaite).

Today, Grubay's former residence and Nurse Radix's residence stand as replicas of the past. The paint on what is left of the house where Grubay lived seems eager to free itself from the walls, but the frame remains intact. The house is left bare, and no curtains cover the abuse it sustained during Hurricanes Ivan and Emily.

Left abandoned, it reminds us of what it once was: a colosseum like that of Rome, occupied by a gladiator named Grubay. It was through this window that we heard Mother on the inside, pounding her piano, hitting notes unrelated to each other, and playing songs only recognizable to her ears. Mother did not care what those on the outside heard or thought of her chopping. She did her thing, and that was all that mattered.

Through this window, we heard Grubay speaking to one of his children: "If one plus one is two, and two plus two is four, then three plus three must be f----- six!" He was not being abusive; that was just Grubay's manner of speaking.

The window served another purpose. Grubay would peep through it to measure the crowd size on the seaside wall, next to the flowerpot, beside his truck. The truck driver's name was Akada.

On many Saturday nights, we packed into the truck, like sacks of cement, as Akada drove us to BBC nightclub.

Grubay, after his furtive scanning of the crowd on the seaside, would emerge to deliver one of his signatures stories. And when he did, our laughter filled the air from Cooper Hill to Old Fort. We had come to accept his stories as tall tales but never as lies.

Nurse Radix: "The Deliverer"

Her home is like a broken skeleton. With moss and dew and rust—and battered by the sea salt of the waters of the Carenage—it is nothing compared to what it once was. No one will ever guess that, once upon a time, within the walls of that house, Nurse Radix lived on the pregnant curve of the Wharf.

The entrance to Leo Janet's house is now known as "the Ghetto." From my boyhood memories, Leo Janet was a robust, redskin man with a powerful voice. By some estimations, he had enough in his pocket to attract those of the opposite sex and ensure his social security would be taken care of in ill health or death. Folks back then kept their money close to their elbows, below their mattresses, and in unsuspecting crevices of their houses. Sou Sou, however, was their preference, their choice, of "banking" and saving. Sou Sou was a merry-go-round system where the recipient would pay a small fee upon receipt of a "hand" or payout, and that was as far as they trusted their money to spin without fear. The "Penny Bank"—today's Grenada Co-operative Bank on Church Street—began to introduce them to a system they once saw as designed and designated only for the plantocracy and privileged.

Nurse Radix, or "Nurse" as she was commonly known, was a household name on the Wharf, Park Lane, Green Street, Tyrell Street, and Cooper's Hill. Her name rang as much as the Anglican church bell, which she was able to see and hear from her front window. Her white midwife uniform dignified her ethnicity. Hardly any woman who was pregnant or in labor needed to scamper to the general hospital to deliver their baby when Nurse Radix was around.

We owe Nurse Radix a great deal of gratitude. My hope is that a fitting honor will be bestowed in her name someday as one who brought many into this world safely. It's quite unfortunate that it already hasn't been done, considering the families and households who, at one time or another, took up residence around and in close proximity to Nurse Radix's home.

The Ghetto is far from that today. When queries are made of Nurse Radix, we can tell others about her. She was of the Wharf—and she was from the Wharf. Everyone knew Nurse Radix as "the Deliverer."

The Man: Leon (Tomkeen)

HE WAS A spirited but chirpy with the swiftness of a magician; this talent made him a resource center for item seekers. If you needed it, Tomkeen would find it and provide it for you. He was never known to be a stevedore, but he could always be seen on the docks or in the vicinity of the cargo ships as they unloaded their goods. He walked briskly, and he always had a mischievous and conniving grin on his face. His body weight invariably shifted whenever he left the premises of the port.

The wrappings around his waist could vary from the least expected to that which was requested. If a customs officer or a guard approached him while he was leaving the docks, he would say in a loud voice, "*Boy*, don't touch me!" He would start taking off his trousers—exposing himself—knowing very well that whatever items he had taken were hidden in a place where he would be able to retrieve them later. If he had items around his waist, the same threat would be made with some hesitation, prompting the guards to quickly usher him out to avoid another bare-bottom moment.

He taunted our parents too, and he invited us to view some of the erotic magazines he carried in his back pocket. As young boys, we looked forward to the viewings each time he waved one in his hands. Tomkeen was truly a piece of the fabric that made the quilt of the Wharf a tapestry of beauty.

Leon (Tomkeen).

The Women from the Wharf Who Made A Difference

THE WHARF MAY never be archived among the historical places and sites like Paris and the Eiffel Tower, Rome and the Coliseum, India and the Taj Mahal; London and Trafalgar Square and Big Ben, or New York and the Statue of Liberty. Nonetheless, what we did have on the Wharf were people who made an impact and a difference in our lives as young men. The young women were not as visible then, and we understood why.

They included the Brathwaites (Brother B and his wife "Titter"), Mr. Hezzy and Miss Agnes, Nurse Radix, Miss Coard, Ma Fletcher, Ms. Harbin, LH, Ms. Lorna, Mr. Thomas (Bells) and his wife, the Renwick (Bernardine family), Stroude and LaHee families. A list too lengthy to mention them all. Most have transitioned to the great beyond, including Ms. Omega. She was a matriarch, a stalwart, a pillar of the Wharf community. Ms. Omega loved going to the movies and reading comic books—from *Archie* to *Sad Sack*. Her children became an integral part of the Wharf community and made their contributions as steelpan musicians and sportsmen. She loaned them to us over the years: Hudson (Bapp), Spanky (pannist/arranger/tuner). Michael (Boose), Elvis (Sisco), and others. In steelband and sports, they made Panasonic, Angel Harps, and Carenage United forces to be reckoned with in their heyday.

Other than Spanky, I had the pleasure of playing with Ms. Omega's son Michael (Boose) Cyrus. He was one of the youngest, most talented, most creative arrangers of my time. As with Empire, Ms. Omega has left us, but she will never be forgotten.

Miss Omega

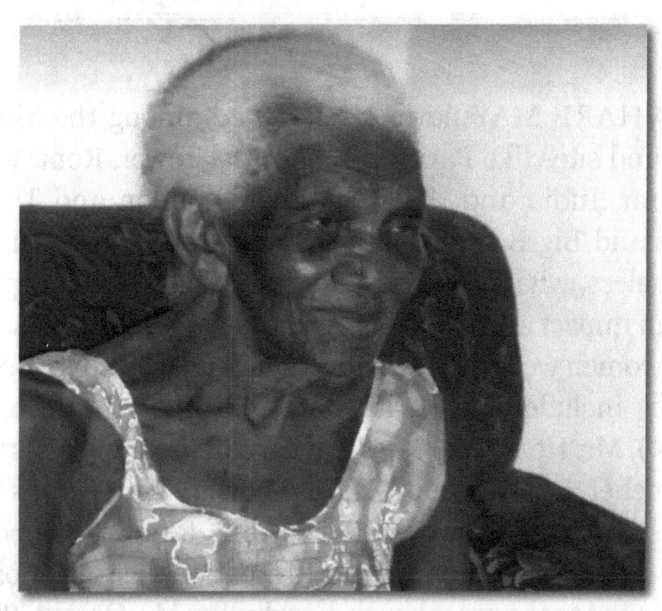

82

Mammy Fletch

Iris "Mammy Fletch" (Cheryl Fletcher).

IRIS FLETCHER, OR "Mammy Fletch" as she was commonly known, was the person who encouraged the regrouping of Angel Harps after they found themselves in the valley of despair in 1969. She was an avid supporter of the band and commanded maximum respect from the Wharf boys. They sometimes displayed unruliness with their tongues and their fists. She was another female stalwart.

Roslind "Baby" Greenidge

Most people knew her as "Baby," and her support of Angel Harps was unwavering. She never failed to criticize the pan players when she found something not up to par or out of line whether with their song arrangements or behavior. Baby and George Croney were inseparable as a couple—until he migrated to the United States in 1968. Her invaluable support and encouragement were instrumental in shaping the lives of many young Angel Harps players. The band paid tribute to Baby at her homegoing—a well deserving act of gratitude for Roslind "Baby" Greenidge.

Pamela "Pam" Steele

ONE CAN'T SPEAK of the Wharf without mentioning Pamela "Pam" Steele. She is authentically and genuinely a "Wharf girl," and she would not stammer when proudly telling of her relationship, attachment, and connection to the community. Pam is a fountain of knowledge and information—far beyond what anyone could imagine. She is an archivist, chronologist, genealogist, hagiographer, geographer, theorist, and philologist—and many more titles could be added to her name, including career public servant.

Pam worked in public service for more than thirty-six years and rose to the rank of permanent secretary. She is also a veritable steeple in the Anglican church. Her involvement in all aspects of the Anglican ministry is unquestionably of value to the church family. More importantly, she is a diehard supporter of Angel Harps and the carnival mas bands that emerged from the Wharf.

Pam is a Wharf girl from the "Carnival Bungalow" and a "Wharf girl to the bone." Ask her, and she will tell you.

Pamela "Pam" Steele:
The "Doyenne" of the Wharf

Empire: The Glory Days of House, Pit, Balcony, and Box

PRIOR TO FINDING employment and becoming salaried workers—men now earning a "change"—we did whatever was necessary to secure a fee for matinee, which is what we called going to the movies. It was matinee—whether in the daytime, evening, or nighttime, totally ignoring the strict definition of that word "matinee."

For an unemployed youth, a matinee fee—even just a few cents—was extremely difficult to muster. The available avenues to acquire the required sum were odd jobs, including diving off the jetty or into the harbor to retrieve coins thrown overboard from cruise liners by tourists.

We also "stole from God," keeping—and not passing along—the pennies given for "church collection" on Sundays. Alternatively, we subjected ourselves to the abuse of others, begging them for change to help with the movie fee.

House and balcony seats in the movie theater were beyond our pockets. The pit was our habitat, and it was where men unleashed their tirades when a movie unraveled or went "bust" (as we called it). Bad words and unsavory words were lobbed at those in the operating room behind the balcony.

When we did not have the money to purchase tickets, many of us waited until intermission to chance our luck at getting into the theater without paying. We tried blending in with the paying patrons who had exited at intermission and were reentering the movie house after refreshing themselves and picking up a quick snack from Brofitt or from Ms. Baby Shop. If you were not careful, because of slowness in service, you could miss most of the second half the movie.

We did blend in frequently and made our way past the gatekeepers—except for Big Bear (Mr. Rupert Williams). He had a knack for finding those who were attempting illegal, nonpaying entry or trying to "scheme in" without paying. We avoided playing our tricks on Big Bear because of his temper. Bear would not hesitate to let you feel his oversized hand behind your head. Other memorable "ticket tearers" for the pit included "Mas Man" Edmond Christopher, Gerald Greenidge, Mr. Jones, and Texaco. Mr. Greenidge sold the tickets for the pit in a booth at the top of the steps, which exited onto Tyrrel Street and served as a shortcut for those who lived in the Cocoa and on Goat Hill. The ticket sales were sometimes slow, but there was always a rush to see the spaghetti westerns. We called the Chinese thrillers "Wang Yu movies," including *The One-Armed Swordsman, The Way of the Dragon,* and *Game Of Death. The Sound of Music* carried the flagship for the best musical.

Mr. Greenidge was unable to keep his eyes open for any length of time. I am not sure if it was because of exhaustion from his nine-to-five job or if it was "dropsy." Mr. Greenidge's sleepiness encouraged some guys to endeavor to get their hands through the small cubbyhole of the ticket booth to retrieve the cash from the sale of tickets. None of the would-be thieves was ever successful—not even "Fox" when he tried fishing out the cash by using bamboo rods with glue, gum, and tar at the ends.

Another variable in the pit was the art of eating a snack without sharing. Without mastering the art, your small bag of groundnut may have to be shared with an entire bench of movie-watching friends. You could not allow anyone to know you had a prized possession like a bag of groundnut or – as we say in the Grenada lingo - "crappo would smoke your pipe".

The Classics

AS YOUNG MEN growing up in Grenada, we regularly went to the movies. It was a calling. We categorized some films as "must-see flicks," including *Rio Bravo, The Learning Tree, Cooley High, The Great Escape, The Magnificent Seven, Quo Vadis, To Hell and Back, Rio Bravo, Shane,* and *PT 109*. For the musical category, *Sounder*—with Cicely Tyson and Paul Winfield—and *The Sound of Music* deserve a special place on the ratings scale.

Pan in We Blood

"Hell-Cats Steel Orchestra" (George "Malaki" Johnson, *National Geographic*).

Trinidad and Tobago pan pioneer Elliot "Ellie" Mannette:

Fitzpatrick "Sheepy" Belgrave.

STEELPAN, A TWENTIETH-CENTURY musical invention, was synonymous with the Wharf and its surroundings. The "gift" and the "gifted" emerged from Lucas Street, Green Street, Park Layne, the Cocoa, Goat Hill, Tanteen, and the Wharf. There were steelbands such as Hell Cats, GASSPO, and Troubadours. Harp Tones—under the captaincy of Mosley Parks—ushered in Teensville, which was founded by Charles Moses and Walter "Dictator" Thomas.

Harp Tones and Teensville, though not making the expected impact, set a path for other community bands such as such

Photo credit: Karl Otway: Harp Tones - Mosley Parks (Brother of George Croney)

Angel Harps and Panasonic. Steve "Spanky Bapp" Cyrus led a group of others in the formation of Panasonic in the Cocoa, in the vicinity of Cooper's Hill area, and a few feet from Tyrrel

Street. Spanky's Panasonic was formed in the mid-1960s; but a new group, a new Panasonic, emerged in the latter part of the 1960s. Angel Harps came into being after the return to Grenada of George Croney. He and a few Grenadian expatriates had been living in "South," which is what we called Trinidad back then.

Teensville's Charles Moses and Walter Thomas—with a contingent of young men from Springs and Woburn—joined up with George Croney's pan side (steelband) on the Wharf, which he named Angel Harps. Harp Tones members were also incorporated into Angel Harps.

George's intention with the newly formed Angel Harps was to have a band in Grenada that was good as any band in South. He was the founder, the tuner, the arranger, and the captain of that band until his departure in 1968. A very quiet individual, George possessed an unmistakable flair in attire. His clothes were casual but noticeable. It was not done deliberately to impress anyone; that was just the man. He brought that dapper appearance from South; most of the early Harps men, the founding members, displayed the look with pride. Their "threads," ranging from Chinese vests to Converse sneakers, arrived on wooden schooners that trafficked in agricultural produce between Trinidad and Grenada.

George, by nature, was the reticent type, but he was not one you wanted to have a confrontation with. A highlight of George's remarkable brilliance came to fruition in 1967 when the band entered the Panorama competition as "Shell Angel Harps." The National Steelband Festival was held at the Reno Cinema. As the band's "test piece" selection, George chose to play an excerpt from *Carmen*. The composition by the French maestro Georges Bizet premiered in France on March 3, 1875.

Angel Harps' other festival song, "Calypso of Choice," was "67" by Lord Kitchener. The same calypso piece was played in competition in Trinidad by the great Guinness Cavaliers. Listening to the renditions of "67" by Guinness Cavaliers and

Angel Harps, it is my firm opinion that George came very close to what he and the others intended to achieve. Angel Harps won the overall Steelband Festival title and the solo title as well. This sent a message to the other steelbands in Grenada that there was a new sound in town. That was a clear statement in sound and style and the beginning of Angel Harps as an institution. It was George Croney's Angel Harps.

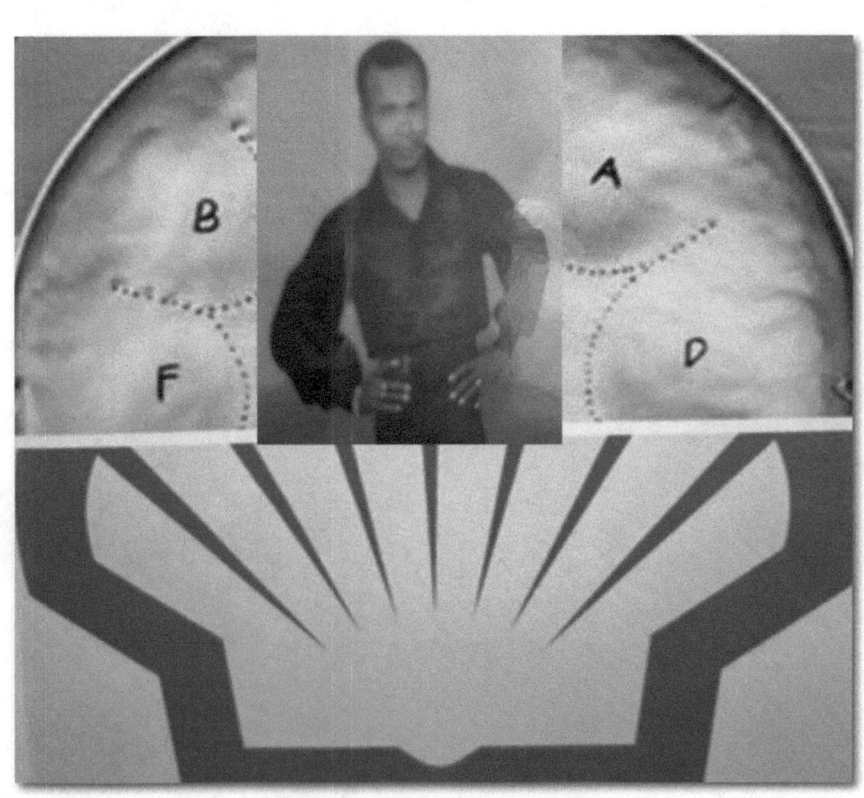

SHELL ANGEL HARPS

A few original members of Angel Harps.

The 1968 Steelband Festival at the Reno Cinema and Dixieland from Carriacou (Bill Cameron).

Coca-Cola Wayside Steel Orchestra.

Coca-Cola Commancheros Steel Orchestra.

George Croney's Split with Angel Harps

IN 1968, GEORGE Croney parted ways with Angel Harps. In addition to being the tuner of the band, he had the coveted titles of captain and arranger. He was an exceptional talent, a rare breed, by today's standards.

What caused the split between George and the band is still not known. Because he was the "Trinitarian" of Angel Harps, no one had the authority to stop him from dispersing of the pans as he saw fit. It is said that Clayton (alias "Drown"), was the only person rewarded by George with a pan for his hard work. In George's pan tuning, "Drown" served as an assistant. He would sink and prepare the oil drums for tuning.

The disruption between George and Angel Harps forced the band to rely on another tuner. In 1969, Angel Harps turned to Brother Broff. At the time, his experience as a tuner was relegated only to that of tuning tourists' souvenir steelpans.

Around the same time, Panasonic—a relatively new steelband from the Cocoa—was attracting some young players to the orchestra, including myself. The others who formed the nucleus of Panasonic included Maga, Orlando, Fraser, Willard (Kalaky), Zack Bernard, Pirate, Max Harbin, and Michael "Boose" Cyrus. We were eager to play pan—any pan.

Panasonic did not have any organized structure as I can recall, but the band got gigs here and there, which brought elation to us as young players. Panasonic, I would say, was owned by Steve "Spanky Bapp" Cyrus. Like George Croney of Angel Harps, Spanky was the tuner and arranger. Willard

"Kalaky," a versatile and skilled pannist, also played a role as arranger.

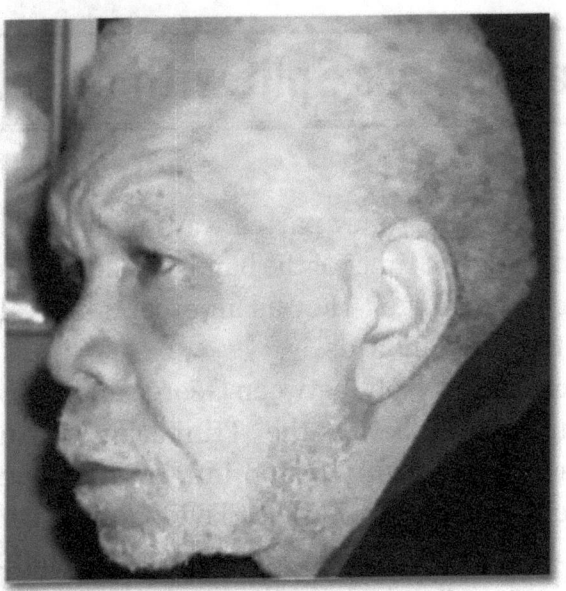

Panasonic founder, tuner, and arranger Steve "Spanky Bapp" Cyrus.

Angel Harps tuner, Brother Broff (Panorama 1969).

There were two principal avenues through which Angel Harps and Panasonic obtained the drums that they converted into musical instruments. In one instance, the drums were provided courtesy of Bruce Bain. Bain, known as "Skipper Bruce" or

"Spider," worked at the electricity power station, which was owned and controlled by the British-based Commonwealth Development Corporation (CDC). There is a plant, named after Bain, at what's now Grenlec at Queen's Park.

In the second instance, it's still a wonder no one ever went to jail for channeling drums to the bands. The drums were stolen at night. As Panasonic began bearing fruits and developing, the pans under Spanky began disappearing. They were being sold to fledgling bands. Spanky was a talented pan musician and an excellent tuner, and he was quickly approaching the caliber of Wilfred Harris, the national tuner of Grenada. Why Angel Harps did not lean on Harris as their tuner had much to do with pride—at the expense of tone. Harris was a former member of Wayside Steel Orchestra from River Road, and Wayside was the nemesis of Angel Harps. Contracting Harris as tuner would have been blasphemous.

Eventually, like George Croney, Spanky emigrated from Grenada. A new tuner and a new arranger were needed. For musical arranging, the band utilized the services of Kalaky and Trevor Emmanuel. We called him "Father" because he was a Roman Catholic priest.

Panasonic benefited from another attempt at a community steelband that was initiated by Napoleon "Napp" McBurnie. Many of the young panmen who transitioned to Panasonic and Angel Harps acquired their skills and mentorship from that small band on Park Lane. Napp's band was located next to his home on Park Lane and practiced in an unused garage. It was widely considered to be an apprenticeship steelband learning program. Napp later migrated to Florida, and he resided there until his passing. In Florida, he played with George Croney—who had also taken up permanent residence there.

Napoleon "Napp" McBurnie.
Bottom picture: Napp, Smeckmeck, and George.

Panasonic (David) Goes Up against Angel Harps (Goliath)

IN 1969, PANASONIC saw an opportunity to compete against the biggest and best band in the nation, Angel Harps. A bitter feud had developed among some key supporters of Angel Harps. They shifted their focus, support, and attention to us—the rookie steelband musicians of Panasonic—hoping to teach Angel Harps a lesson.

Some of the main characters in that feud were Winston "Shitty" and "Monarchy" Bain. As youngsters, we had no knowledge of what had transpired to create this disagreement in the pan movement on the Wharf, and we were not interested in asking or finding out. Whatever it was, it was "big people business". All we cared about was the attention directed at us—including food and drinks—and their making us believe we were the best thing after leaven bread.

"Shitty" and "Monarchy," in a heightening of the taunting with their new rivals, decided to move Panasonic from on top of the hill in the Cocoa to the passageway, between the Lime Factory and the LaHee's residence. That passageway was known as George Street. Ironically, that location was just a spit away from Angel Harps and their panhouse, which was situated in the Coals Market, next to the Phoenix Cigarette Factory.

The Angel Harps/Panasonic feud reminded me of a political campaign. Posters were prepared and hung, and threats and name-calling went back and forth. The animosity between the Coals Market Band and the George Street Band was as thick as the fumes emanating from the Lime Factory. However, there were no physical altercations; both sides knew where to draw the lines.

Going into Panorama in 1969, we were delighted in knowing that we sounded sweeter and better than Harps. Never in our wildest dreams did we—the biblical Davids—think it was possible to defeat Harps. They were the Goliaths of pan. On Panorama Night, Angel Harps played Kitchener's "Bull." Commancheros from St. Paul's performed "The Good, the Bad, and the Ugly." Two selections were required of steelbands participating in Panorama in those days, but I can't recall the other songs played by the bands.

Panasonic made an unorthodox choice of taking a classical piece, *Aida*, and transposing it into a calypso tempo.

Trevor Emmanuel on Grand Anse Beach with members of South Stars Steel Orchestra.

Infamous George Street.

The song was arranged by Father Trevor Emmanuel—he was still a Catholic priest at the time—and Panasonic came away as Panorama champions that night. Angel Harps pointed their fingers at Chris Checkley and his Charlie Chaplin speed on the "tumba" for their loss. You will never hear any member of that band of Angel Harps (1969) crediting the skillful arrangement of Trevor Emmanuel or us—the young pannists of Panasonic—for the flogging they received that night. They often said, "They did not beat us—we beat ourselves." What a bunch of crap!

Eventually, the feud between Harps and Panasonic subsided—and the animosity disappeared. By July 1969, the youthful champions began the process of integrating into the big boys' band (Angel Harps). They joined forces with the more experienced and seasoned players to compete in the coveted National Steelband Festival carded for December of that same *year.

Panasonic Steel Orchestra.

In the Coals Market, a few former Panasonic Steel Orchestra musicians—now full-fledged members of the "baddest" band in the land—were ad-libbing on pans made by Brother Broff. We were not practicing for a special gig or function; as youngsters, it was just for the love of pan. Our desire was simple; we wanted to remain the best by practicing ceaselessly. Our aim was always to record a Grenada steelband album, the first of its kind, but it was not necessarily for the purpose of bragging. We thought we were as good as the bands from Trinidad and Tobago that had produced many recordings.

A stranger casually sauntered in the direction of the Coals Market Panhouse. Lloyd Gaye came to the mainland after visiting relatives in Carriacou. With his head leaning slightly to the left and speaking in a very soft tone, he asked who the captain of the band was, indicating that he was a pan tuner from Trinidad. This was confirmed when someone handed him a pair of double tenor sticks. He effortlessly ran a scale with the smoothness that only a specialist panman would have been able to master. At the time, many of the senior players were working on the docks as stevedores.

ANGEL HARPS PSYCHEDELIC SAILOR 1970

Clevroy "Depo" DePradine

I can't remember who gave Lloyd the go-ahead to tune a double tenor sitting in the corner of the panhouse, which was the usual storage area for tenor pans. Many claimed it was the late drummer, Ming, who gave Lloyd the green light to tune the double tenor. Lloyd went to work, carefully moving his hammer and tuning the pan. On completion, when we heard the tonal quality, we knew that was the beginning of a new sound for Angel Harps.

Lloyd Gay, Dunbar Gibbs, Bertrand "Brother B" Bridgeman, and Carlye "Red Boy" Sylvester.

Sons of the Brave

ANGEL HARPS, STATIONED inside the Coals Market on the Wharf, with the Phoenix Cigarette Factory wall as a backdrop, regrouped under the leadership of Lester Boyke, after the orchestra's defeat to Panasonic—the fledgling steelband from "The Cocoa." Why it was called "The Cocoa" is still unknown; we only knew of one cocoa tree in the area. All the others were located around the vicinity of Marryshow Pasture.

With Lester as captain, Harps redeemed itself in December 1969 at the Regal Cinema by capturing the Steelband Festival title, including first place for best soloist.

In January 1970, Angel Harps began preparation for the Panorama Steelbands Competition. They were determined not to allow a repeat of the previous year. With the youngsters from Panasonic as members of the "Goliath of Steelbands" Angel Harps, that was highly unlikely. Steelbands, back then, were required to play two selections, but it was not necessarily a calypso. Familiarity of the songs mattered, and there were risks in deviating from the norm. There was the danger of not receiving acceptance from the judges for nonconformity.

"Maggie," a song by Lord Kitchener, was selected by Harps as their calypso of choice. For their second selection, the band decided to take a different route. Harps settled on "Sons of the Brave," a classical marching song. Lester asked Ronald "Mitchie" Bain to arrange the marching song. Mitchie, to his credit, had arranged "The Holy City" for Angel Harps the previous year for the band's victory in the Steelbands Festival.

Ronald "Mitchie" Bain.

Mitchie did not hesitate to take up the challenge of arranging the song suggested. Lester, had previously heard the Police Band playing that classical march, "Sons of the Brave" - He did not, at the time, knw the title of the song, but was able to whistle a few bars to Mitchie, a trumpeter in the Police Band. Mitchie immediately recognized and identified the song as "Sons of the Brave" by Thomas Bidgood. Mitchie later admitted that his first choice for the competition would have been the "Tancredi Overture" by Gioachino Rossini. However, at the time, he did not mention this to Lester. He said he was glad he did not.

"Sons of the Brave" became a signature piece on the album *Brighter Out of Darkness*. The recording was another first for Harps and the steelband movement in Grenada.

Rehearsals indicated that Harps meant business. Before Panorama, one problem lingered. What should the band wear on the night of Panorama? Arthur and Lester discussed the issue on Ma Coard's veranda and decided on appearing as Spiritual Baptists. The band took to the stage dressed as

Baptists. The cloth had been bought in Miss Wallace's store (Wallace Jookdown).

To add intrigue to the unorthodoxy of the outfit, Cosley Boyke (the brother of Lester) came on stage, rang a bell, and lit two candles. Rumors began to spread—by the losers—that Angel Harps had worked obeah to win Panorama. We knew, without a doubt, that Angel Harps did not work obeah to win; they were truly the "sons of the brave."

Angel Harps, dressed like Spiritual Baptists, practicing before taking the stage at Panorama Night 1970 (Lester Boyke and Arthur Coard).

Angel Harps Loses Panorama and Band of the Year - Walter "Dictator" Thomas captures Calypso Title (69)

In the Caribbean, there's an island,
Found and set aside by nature's plan.
It's so beautiful to see, really,
The Spice Island of the West.
And in the West Indies, I say Grenada please,

Overwhelmingly glad we are to be our country.
Foreigners have recommended it highly,
Hand in hand for a better land,
A people who can understand.
That's business,
Brighter out of Darkness.

Walter "Dictator" Thomas wearing his crown and playing his pan.

Walter "Dictator" Thomas in his senior years, still thrilling audiences with *Brighter Out of Darkness*.

Arthur Bowen and Angel Harps: Man on a Mission or a Mercenary

IN 1968, ARTHUR Bowen, a white man, came to Grenada from either Canada or the United States with the blessings of Uncle Gairy. He was a short, stocky man, and he wore nothing but short khaki pants and sandals—and the bottom button of his shirt was always undone. The button was unable to withstand his oversized stomach.

To us, Bowen's demeanor was suspect; he seemed more like a Mafia man seeking sanctuary in the Caribbean than an accomplished architect, which his resume claimed. Premier Gairy put the Expo 1969 project in the hands of Bowen. Slowly and methodically, he began to draw himself closer and closer to Angel Harps in the Coals Market.

As the Expo project continued, the cottages erected at the south of the island needed painters. Coincidently or conveniently, Bowen employed the boys from Harps to do the painting. He hired them as painters for projects related to Expo, carpenters, and watchmen! Can you imagine the guys from Angel Harps as watchmen? Bowen, however, got the job done. Expo 69 was a success—even when others doubted the project and considered it an impossible task.

In 1969, the band took a boat, the *Simstrand,* to Carriacou. The visit to the sister isle of Grenada was an experience of hardship that we will never forget. It was horrific! We had no money and very little to eat. The three days we spent on the island were pure hell. Between 1969 and 1970, something went down between Bowen and Gairy; Bowen became enemy number one. Gairy was definitely onto something.

We were invited to a certain individual's home for a meeting that—in our youthful innocence—we believed was to discuss pan business. To our surprise, instead of a steelpan discussion, Bowen and a tall, light-skinned politician from Tanteen—whose name I choose not to mention—talked about overthrowing Uncle. We, the young panmen of Harps, did not wait to hear how the meeting ended. It wasn't long after the meeting that Gairy issued instructions to deport Bowen—despite him having a Grenadian wife.

As with Lloyd Gay, fingers were pointed at Ming as the person who brought Bowen into the Coals Market and introduced him to Angel Harps.

Lincoln "Ming" Andrews.

Two Rebels in White

TREVOR EMMANUEL WAS still in the seminary when he decided to give up his priestly vocation for a vice, which surely tormented him at the time. Many could not understand the logic of this transition from piety to pan. He exchanged mass for mas and the penance of a saint for a pariah to the path to "heaven" and the "promised mansions."

Panhouses were never constructed to be confession booths, and playing pan was never intended to be a private space for sinners to admit their transgressions to their spiritual leaders, priests, or pastors. Father Trevor Emmanuel risked going to heaven for that magnetic vice of pan music. Father Malligan or Mulligan was the other "rebel in white", and for the sake of expediency, I will stick with the name that rings most in my ear: Malligan.

We suspected he came from England or Ireland, but that was immaterial to us on the Wharf. It was his bravery as a man of the cloth, venturing to establish a community center in a place where a church was needed.

Unlike Father Emmanuel, Malligan did not play pan. He thought establishing a "vagabond center" on the Wharf would be more effective than engaging in a steelband. The center was directly responsible for many people becoming very proficient at table tennis, billiards, pool, Chinese checkers, and dominoes. The money collector at the center, acting on behalf of Father Malligan, was Arthur Monroe.

Father Malligan. Trevor Emmanuel.

Father Malligan, I'm certain, would have heard every discolored adjective from the lips of those he hoped would eventually experience miraculous transformations. He got used to the verbal steam from the agitated vagabonds and never allowed them to intimidate him. It is imperative that the names of Father Emmanuel and Father Malligan, the two "rebels in white," are a fixture of Wharf history. Their stories are an integral part of the collage of the Wharf.

A Bold Move: The Saints and the Scoundrels

IT WAS A time when playing pan was seen as a defiant act against the establishment and a noisy societal nuisance that attracted vagabonds and thugs. This stereotype was not limited to Trinidad, the incubation chamber where pan was invented. This negative imagery was present in Grenada, and everywhere else, as attempts were made to set up steelbands as a form of entertainment.

Pan music and the players of the instrument were never viewed as ideal citizens. The early clashes between steelbands in Trinidad—and to a limited extent in Grenada—did not help dispel the notion of thuggery. Some may say the perception was warranted. These early territorial pan rivalries saw a variety of weapons used in the clashes: projectiles like broken bottles and stones, cutlasses, knives, and switchblades. Unhelpful, too, were the unflattering names of some well-known badjohns— such as Shark, Cobo-Jack, Snakehead, and Raybone—and their frequent encounters with the police. All of this reinforced the negatives about pan and panmen. This very point was captured in a 1950s calypso, "Steelband Clash," which was sung by Carlton Joseph, calypsonian Lord Blakie:

It was a bacchanal, in fifty Carnival
Fight for so with Invaders and Tokyo
Mi friend run and left his hat
Wen dey hit him with a baseball bat
Never me again, to jump in a steelband in Port of Spain

Invaders beating sweet, coming up a street
Tokyo coming down beating very slow
And friends wen the two bands clash
Mama-yo if yu see cutlass
Never me again to jump in a steelband in Port of Spain

In 1971, many heads turned in astonishment when Angel Harps acquiesced to a request to teach the art of playing pan to a contingent of schoolgirls from the St. Joseph's Convent (SJC) in St. George's. This bold request was initiated by Regan Nedd, an accomplished musician at SJC and leader of the school's choir. I remain unsure whether this intrepid step had the blessings of Mother Superior—Sister Gertrude—but Regan made the request.

Regan's entreaty initiated a first for Angel Harps; a first for Grenada, and the beginning of smashing that widely held perception of steelband men as untouchables. It happened because a courageous young student from St. Joseph's Convent dared to venture into the unknown where the unsaved resided.

After a few lessons, it became difficult to distinguish, in playing skills, between Angel Harps (the band) and the female students they were tutoring. The SJC protégés performed with us at a few fundraising concerts at the Regal Cinema and, to the delight of the spectators, at sporting events at Queen's Park. This was the beginning and acceptance of something unheard of: an unprecedented act of gallantry by these convent girls breaking the ceiling of mistrust and misunderstanding.

The keen eyes of Sister Gertrude never left or winked for a moment during their stint with us. In 2000, at an Angel Harps reunion, the former students were recognized with the "Pioneer Award." They were also recognized at the band's fiftieth-anniversary celebrations in 2015.

Regan Nedd-Mendes
Christine Francis-Clarkson

Michaele Hercules
Hazel Hurley-Bierzynski
Jenny-Lyn Preudhomme-Cherman
Jennifer Gairy
Cecilia John-Ouedraogo
Annette Phillip-Cunningham
Brenda Coard
Maureen Coard
Marlene Noel

In 1973, Angel Harps registered its first full-time female pannist, Antonia Bernard. As a member of Angel Harps Steel Orchestra, she likely also was first female to participate on a stage with a Grenada steelband.

Antonia also accompanied the band when it traveled to record its second steelband album, *As Prescribed*. Antonia Bernard helped smash the ceiling of the local pan movement, and she was recognized by Angel Harps at their 2000 reunion and the fiftieth anniversary.

Regan Nedd—Mendes (at left) conducting New Dimensions in preparation for the 2005 Steelband Festival in New York. Pioneers Award presented at Angel Harps 2000 Awards Ceremony: Michaele Hercules, Jenny-Lyn Preudhomme-Cherman, Cecilia John-Ouedraogo, Regan Nedd-Mendes,

Sister Gertrude

Antonia Bernard.

After the Angel Harps/SJC program ended, Panasonic Steel Orchestra continued the steelband mentorship and tutoring with another group of young ladies from the SJC St. George's. Among the Panasonic tutors were Trevor Emmanuel, Orlando Thomas, Ulric Fraser, and others. Girls immaculately dressed for a performance at the Regal Cinema.

The Makings of an Album: Brighter Out of Darkness

ANGEL HARPS HAD a renewed sound with Lloyd Gay as the band's regular tuner. They began to move full steam ahead with transforming a dream into reality: the recording of a musical album. Evelyn Ross, as the man at the helm of the project, started making arrangements by reaching out to his contacts in Barbados, which was where *Brighter Out of Darkness* was to be produced.

One of his main contacts in Barbados was the Mottley family, which included Mia Amor Mottley, who was elected prime minister of Barbados on May 25, 2018.

Mr. Ross, Mia Mottley's godfather, was also the best man at her parents' wedding. Mia's grandmother was Grenadian; she spent a lot of time with her and learned much about Grenada.

Brighter Out of Darkness was made possible and given life through the efforts of many, but without the efforts of Evelyn Ross, Lloyd Gay, Lester Boyke, James Clarkson, and Arthur Coard, the album would not have come to fruition.

Angel Harps, between 1970 and 1971, began a series of indoor concerts to raise funds in pursuit of traveling to Barbados to complete the album. These concerts were held primarily on Sunday mornings at the Regal Cinema and were highly successful financially.

Before leaving Grenada, Mr. Ross utilized his Barbadian connection via the Mottley family and was able to secure living arrangements and other necessities for our steelband musicians. So, with Mr. Ross managing our affairs and with his solid ties in Barbados, we were going to Bimsure with a little clout.

Barbados, at that time, was not ready to embrace a bunch of young men with afros as wide as silk cotton trees, oversized trousers, and T-shirts emblazoned with slogans supporting Pan-Africanism, the Black Power movement, and Angela Davis, Stokely Carmichael, and other political activists. Soon after we unloaded our pans on the Bridgetown docks, we were grilled on why we came to Barbados and whether we had any connection with Bobby Clark. The Black Power agitator and sympathizer was fresh out of university like Maurice Bishop, who later became Grenada's prime minister.

We also did not know that the country was about to hold an election. Quite unwittingly, we found ourselves in the midst of a political election campaign, and we became the subjects of political suspicion by some Bajans.

The Harps traveled to Barbados on one of the federal ships that were based in Trinidad. The MV *Federal Maple* and MV *Federal Palm*, gifts from the Canadian government, were launched in 1961. The West Indian Federation was designed to facilitate regional travel and transport cargo among English-speaking Caribbean countries.

The ships carried fifty cabin passengers, two hundred deck passengers, and 1,500 tons of break-bulk cargo. It was ideal for our trip to Barbados since it provided comfortable passenger accommodations and cargo space for our instruments. The service of the ships continued for several years after the collapse of the West Indian Federation in 1962.

BRIGHTER OUT OF DARKNESS

GRENADA ANGEL HARPS STEEL ORCHESTRA
(Panaroma & Festival Champions)

An Angel Harps Sunday-morning concert at Regal Cinema.

Evelyn Ross.

Maestros: James "Wakax" Clarkson and Lester Boyke

PANMEN WERE FULLY aware that we were being left in an unlucky lurch with the departure to Canada of Lester Boyke, a self-taught musician, who was both our captain and arranger.

The void, in arranging in the absence of Lester and in preparation for the album's recording, was filled by James Clarkson and Arthur Coard. Clarkson was a seasoned, trained, qualified musician and bandmaster of the Royal Grenada Police Force Band.

James returned to Grenada around 1970 from Trinidad. He was a member of the Trinidad Regiment and an accomplished maestro for the Trinidad Regiment Band. James, to his credit, also had the opportunity to perform with Catelli All-Stars, one of Trinidad's best steelbands. As arranger, James fostered a marriage with the Harps that has lasted for decades. He was rigorous in practice and traveled with the band to Barbados for the recording of *Brighter Out of Darkness*.

It was a new era, a new sound, as the first steelband in Grenada to produce a high-quality album.

In 1972, history again was made when James Clarkson embarked on a "brass and steel" combination between Angel Harps and the Royal Grenada Police Force Band. Police musicians and pannists set out on a series of island-wide open-air concerts. One of the selections in the "brass and steel" repertoire was Franz von Suppe's classical piece "Poet and Peasant." A few days before the concert tour began, we discovered that the musical key in which Angel Harps was playing and practicing was different from the key of the Police Band. The challenge arose because we, as panmen, played by ear and not by reading the music scores.

Angel Harps had to transpose the music in order to be in musical sync with the Police Band. We did it in a matter of days—thanks to the expertise of James Clarkson and the excellent panmen with whom he worked. Without boasting, we were damn good at what we did. To this day, no other steel orchestra has been in such a collocation and collaboration with brass in a series of concert performances.

Lester Boyke. James Clarkson.

Botanical Gardens: "Brass and Steel." Angel Harps in collaboration with the Police Bands.

The Night Ugly Sam Left Us Standing

SAM BRISTOL—KNOWN BY all as "Ugly Sam"—accompanied Harps to Barbados to complete *Brighter Out of Darkness*. As an "iron man," he was a member of our competent percussion squad.

One night in Barbados, Sam left all of Angel Harps' pretty boys standing on a dance floor in jealousy of him. Band members had taken a break from rehearsing for our recording sessions that were scheduled for the following two days. With the time off, we decided to attend a party at a school on Berbice Road, which was not very far from where we were lodging. Upon entering the party hall, we realized the men outnumbered the women and assumed that being lucky would take precedence over good looks. The chance of that assumption becoming a reality was shattered when a beautiful young lady plucked Sam from the crowd and put her charm on him. We were confused and baffled as to why she chose Sam. They became two in one, inseparable, and they pranced to the spouge ballads of the Merrymen and the Draytons Two.

"You come here to drink milk—or you come here to count cow" was a line from "Drink Milk," a Draytons Two hit. Sam was drinking milk that night and sipping on honey. He was the man—the Casanova of the night—squeezing, grinding, and winking over the young lady's shoulders as if to say to us, "All you taut looks alone matter."

Sam was sailing on the ninth cloud as an angel from Harps. Well, that was all good until the party was over—and Sam decided to "flap his wings" on the young lady. It was then and there that he discovered the beauty who had taken him on the journey wasn't a gorgeous female after all; it was a pretty fella! Fifty years on, Sam's escapade remains a memorable episode in the recording of *Brighter Out of Darkness*.

Enjoying some time off in Barbados

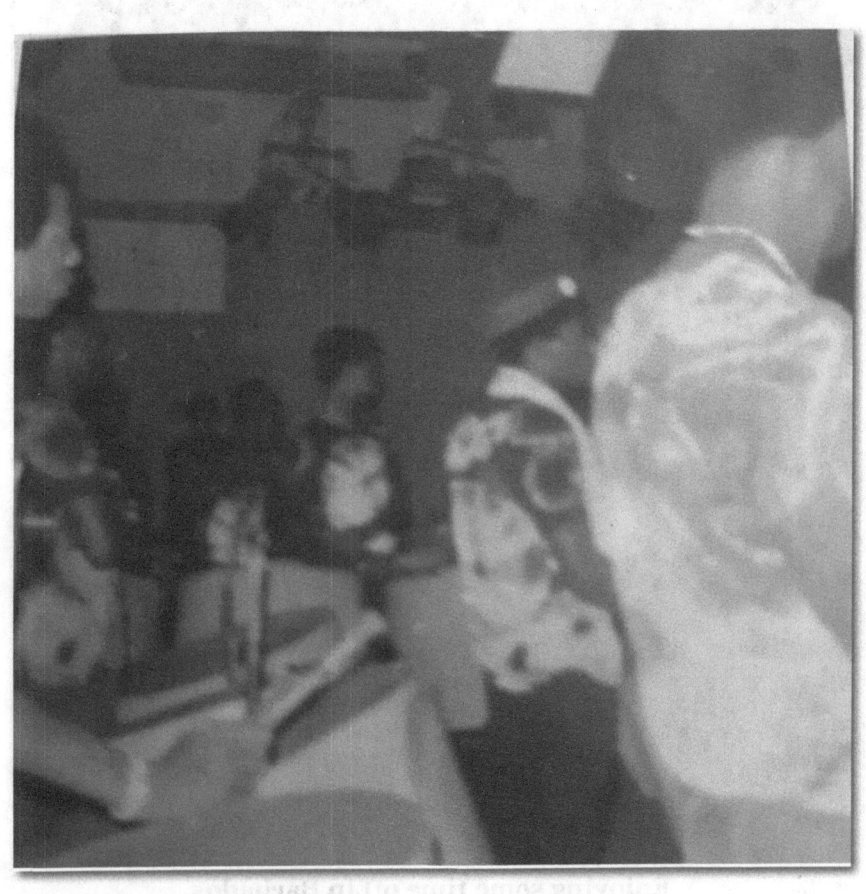

Angel Harps in session

The Many Faces of James "Wakax" Clarkson

Keith "Keithy" Rougier

PRIOR TO AND during the recording of *Brighter Out of Darkness,* Lincoln "Ming" Andrews was the designated drummer of Angel Harps. Ming would be categorized as a "keeping a timing" drummer. There were many who, like Ming, jumped at every opportunity to showcase their skills on the drum set. At the time, "Keithy"—Keith Rougier—played a guitar pan.

After returning from the recording in Barbados, Angel Harps began to challenge themselves with every genre of music under the sun. They included pan renditions of songs such as "Fire" by Osibesa, "Cardova" by the Meters, and "Shaft" by Isaac Hayes. Nothing was untouchable for the Harps, but the band needed a drummer—and not someone who just kept timing. They discovered the desired drummer in Keithy. He ranked high among the best of the popular combo bands in Grenada at the time.

Keithy was agile and versatile, and he was quick on the pedals, snares, cymbals, and crash. He made Angel Harps the envy of other steelbands because he did not simply keep a rhythmic timing. Keithy actually played the drums, and he played superbly. Later on, he joined the Grenada Police Force Band before immigrating to Canada.

Bob on drums.

Another Angel Harps Member Made It on the Big Stage as a Drummer

CARL OTWAY (CARL Vera) is the nephew of George Croney and the son of Mosley Parks, two steelband stalwarts in their own rights. Mosley was the founder of Harp Tones—the band from the Cocoa—and George was the founding captain, arranger, and tuner of Angel Harps. Carl grew up in the yard—Mama's Yard on the Carenage—where George burned, pounded, and tuned his pans. Carl was born with pan sticks in his hands and rhythm in his head. And, though he was never slated as an official drummer for Angel Harps, he and his cousin Marlon were familiar with that percussion instrument. They also executed flawlessly while playing the drums. Carl, before leaving for Canada in the late 1960s, played tenor pan for Harps. Carl was baptized in "the thing."

In Canada, Carl joined a steelband and played at the first Steelbands Panorama in Toronto. He added combo playing to his music passion when he joined Crack of Dawn in 1974 as drummer and vocalist. Carl and Crack of Dawn recorded and performed on stage with Kool and the Gang and other leading American bands. Many still consider Crack of Dawn one of the best soul groups coming out of North America.

Carl standing behind Keithy. Below ; Carl with Crack of Dawn.

The Iron and the Iron Men

Can't imagine any steelband without the sound of the iron
The rims of wheels converted to steels; oh how it feels.
No steelband is quite complete without the sound of the iron.

The cutting, the splicing, the ting-a-ling-ling rattling.
It's the iron that signals to the steelband
One, two, three; are you ready?
No steelband is quite complete without the sound of the iron.

If you're not familiar without the sound of the iron,
You've never been in the engine room of a steelband.
Whether in hand, behind, or on the side of the stand,
No steelband is quite complete without the sound of the iron.

Have you ever seen the expressions on the face of an Iron Man?
How he cuddles the steel in his hand like a woman.
Sweat pouring, eyes burning, undistracted he just keep playing.
Because he knows, no steelband is quite complete without him on the iron.

When Steel Talks.

Angel Harps: Their Flagmen/Women, Engine Room, and Supporters

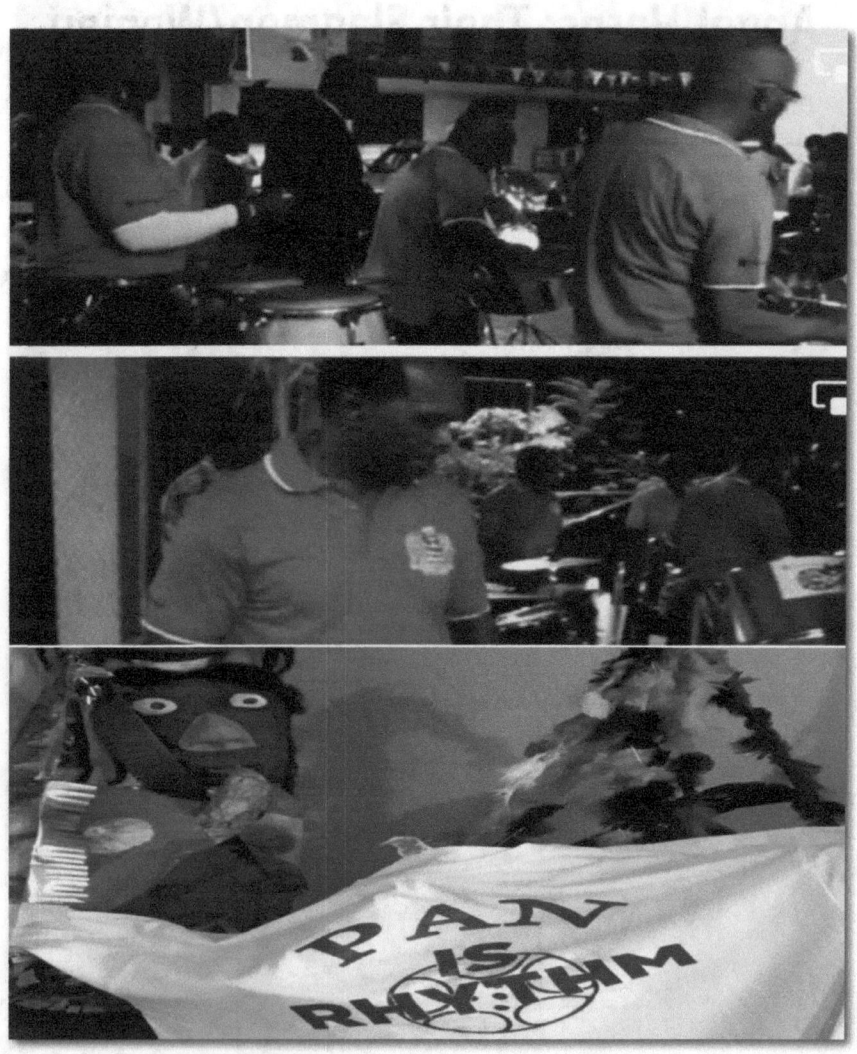

Former Angel Harps stalwarts entertaining at the Angel Harps fiftieth anniversary. (GBTV)

Steelband Men and Nicknames

THE DECADES-LONG ACCOMPLISHMENTS of the Harps are well known. What is not so familiar are the names of the panmen who played for the band—Their Christian names. These names were given to them by their godfathers and godmothers on the day they were brought to the priest to have holy water sprinkled on their foreheads.

Almost everyone associated with Angel Harps—no matter how briefly or remotely connected—came to the band with a nickname or was given one on entering the steel orchestra.

Some names were of biblical characters. Others were movie stars, vagabonds, and Wharf-anointed "saints." In the late sixties, Trevor Emmanuel combined his Catholic clergy duties with arranging music for pan, and the fellas called him "Father." The nickname stayed with Trevor after he left the priesthood.

Here are some of the memorable nicknames: Anasty/Fatman, Air Fish, Bakay, Black Jet, Brother B, Boots, Karl Vera, Tony Poo, Goat, Spanky Bapp, Kalarkie, Brother Broff, Saboo, Zombo, Pumpkinbeard, Drown, Monorchy, Ming, Malutt, Mafu, Money Eye, Maga, Juda, Old Police, Shitty, Shit Soup, Punchy, Judas, Barabas, Redboy, Gun, Gudgin, Crabsauce, James Lickrish, Jazzy, Cockrel, Malu, Chalky, Dupp, Shampoo, Dictator, Max, Bassman, Boose, Barabbas, Jumbie, Ugly Sam, Malutt, Pirate, Nester Boy.

Angel Harps playing at a sporting event in Queen's Park

Angel Harps playing at the Grenada Yacht Club

Former Angel Harps members Houston, Carl "Junk A Lead" Harbin and Austin "Goat" Frederick.

Unique Arrangements and Awards

IN 1973, FOR that year's panorama competition, James Clarkson presented another very difficult piece as "tune of choice" for Angel Harps. The selection, "Dance of the Young Men," tested our fortitude, and the unorthodoxy of the arrangement probed our skillfulness. However, yet again, the Harps prevailed with a complex arrangement, shocking and impressing spectators at the same time with a masterful performance and capturing the panorama championship by a comfortable margin.

James Clarkson was one of several persons recognized in 2015 at the fiftieth-anniversary celebrations of Angel Harps. The Angel Crystal Award—the highest award ever given by Harps for contribution to culture—was presented to Clarkson, Walter St. John, Ronald "Mitchie" Bain, Trevor Emmanuel, Lester Boyke, and Bruce Bain. The late Mosley Parks, George Croney, and Dennis "Away" Lindsay were recognized posthumously with an Angel Crystal Award.

Medal awarded to Angel Harps players at 2000 reunion.

Angel Crystal Award presented at 2000 reunion.

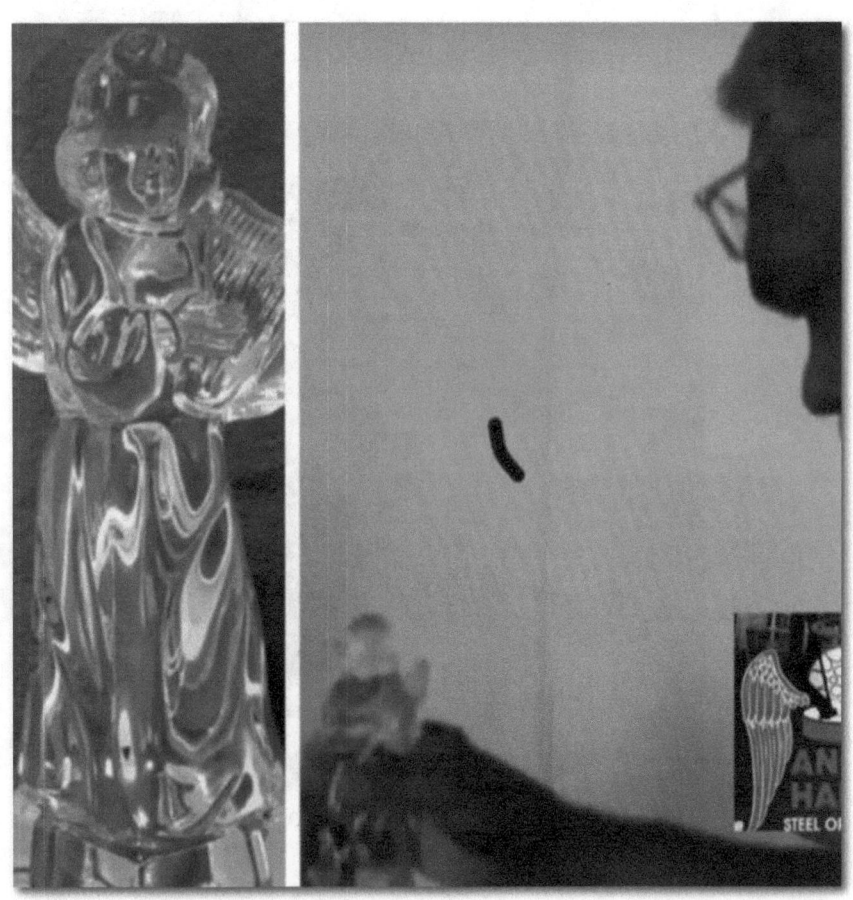
Walter St. John was one of ten recipients of the Angel Crystal Award.

Angel Harps Captain's Award at 2000 reunion.

Kamau, Willie B, CJ, and Depo.

Angel Harps 2000 reunion.

(2015) Angel Harps Awards Ceremony - commemorating their 50th Anniversary.

Sailing into Uncharted Waters

On our way to Barbados on MV *Federal Palm*.

MV *Federal Palm*.

Clarkie and George Coard in Barbados.

The Year the Flamingoes Danced and Harps Played for Royalty

DENNIS "AWAY" LINDSAY was never a panman or a member of Angel Harps like his brother Mossy. However, "Away" was very much identified with the steelband as a masquerade costume producer. His costumed mas' bands included Splendor of Africa and Flag Wavers of Sienna.

Away Lindsay, like George Croney, had made Trinidad his home for a few years. On his return to Grenada, "Away" demonstrated enviable skills and expertise in fashion and styling. A multitalented individual, he was also an accomplished hairstylist.

That that was not all of "Away". He found time, as well, to establish a dance troupe. He conscripted a few members of Angel Harps—Features, Goat, Orlando, Malutt, Maloo and Maga—to be part of The Flamingoes." His dance group performed for Queen Elizabeth and the Duke of Edinburgh at Queen's Park as part of an official tour of the West Indies.

The queen, it is said, was amused at the depictions of royalty she saw on display in Trinidad, but she was stunned and amazed at the acrobatic moves exhibited at Queen's Park by Away's ballet dance troupe. Angel Harps joined the fray and the hype around the visit of the royals with a steelband rendition of "Think, Thanks, Darling, the Queen and the Duke Coming."

Grenadians did not take Premier Eric Matthew Gairy seriously when he proclaimed that Grenada would be sending a contestant to compete in the 1970 Miss World Beauty Pageant. Many dismissed it as just another of Gairy's ambitious urges, forgetting that he had proven the naysayers wrong when they questioned and scoffed at his plans for hosting Expo 69.

Even the most ardent of critics would admit that the exposition, held at True Blue, was a resounding success. Uncle seemed to relish in proving the falsity of his detractors whenever they said, "No, he can't." The Miss World entry was announced with little or no attention from Grenadians. Lo and behold, at midnight on competition day, the adjudicators announced Jennifer Hosten, Miss Grenada, as the new Miss World. A "small-island girl" had smashed the racial ceiling of exclusivity of global beauty pageants. Jennifer defied the odds, and the rest was history.

Pandemonium erupted throughout Grenada and the Caribbean. It was like carnival in the Spice Isle. It was a revolution of beauty, and a contestant from a relatively insignificant Caribbean island, Grenada, captured the coveted title of Miss World 1970 in London.

The announcement of the results, however, wasn't without controversy. Some questioned the presence of Uncle Gairy among the panel of judges. Additionally, a small skirmish broke out in Royal Albert Hall. It was not related to the judges' decision; it was a protest by some referred to as "anarchists." They took issue with women parading themselves in swimsuits. Amid the drama, Jennifer Hosten received her crown from American comedian Bob Hope.

Grenada eagerly awaited the return of Miss World, Jennifer Hosten. Uncle asked Angel Harps to greet the new queen at the airport. Jennifer Hosten's title is one of the few modern events that drew attention to Grenada from the rest of the world. Other attention-grabbing episodes have included the 1979 Revolution, the tragic events of 1983, and Kirani James capturing gold at the 2012 Olympic Games.

So, in 1970 Grenada, while nurses were demonstrating and the agitators were gallivanting against Gairy and his government, Uncle's eyes were on the big stage at the Miss World contest.

What we did not know and—still can't give an answer to—is how Uncle Gairy ended up in the mix of judging such a pageant.

There was no television to view the pageant. Jerry Romain, broadcasting from WIBS radio at Morne Rouge, said, "Jennifer Hosten was crowned Miss World 1970." Buntings and Union Jacks immediately came out of storage—as if Uncle expected the result.

We received word that Uncle wanted Angel Harps to supply pan music to "spice up" Jennifer's homecoming, and we obliged. Jennifer wasn't only our queen; she was Miss World. In a few minutes, we gathered on Grubay's truck and sang, "This is my island, homeland; white sand, sunshine; Grenada, Grenada, Grenada."

Captains, Arrangers and Managers

A TYPICAL SATURDAY ON THE WHARF

THERE WAS NO need for our parents to walk over to the center of St. George—such as to Melville Street and Halifax Street—to shop for fruits and vegetables, bread or fish, or meat. The Wharf was a self-contained shopping center that housed Food Fair and Cold Storage, Coomansingh Shop, Rock N Roll, and Broffit and Harbin Shops. Ms. Gatha sold her cow skin souse, and Ms. Ustin, Ms. Pearl, and Mama Coard sold blood pudding.

The open Coals Market provided enough space for those selling fruits and vegetables. More than half a dozen fishing boats would throttle in with their catch: rock hind, bonito, kingfish, and jacks.

In the Stillness of the Night

It's when in the stillness of the night—in silence,
You will hear the chirping sounds of crickets,
The croaking of the frogs,
And from a distance, a dog may bark.
Provoked or just prowling in the dark.
When the clouds allow, and the stars come out to wink in approval upon this tranquil rock,

Despite the tantrums of men,
Amid the chaos and confusion,
She stands "distinguished" and "august" for us.
Ever asked yourself,
Have you ever considered,
Why is it she is still able to make such an impression on her children,
Causing their hearts to patter when they think of her?
Memories flushed as the crystal rush of Annandale, Mount Carmel, and Concord Falls.
Oh, Grenada!

Carnival Bungalow

MA COARD'S HOUSE was never officially declared a mas' camp; to do so would have somewhat disrespected the home and its residents. However, it was the epicenter of carnival, a place of activities that alerted everyone that carnival was in the air. The ideas for pan and masquerade bands—and the work of shaping, stenciling, painting, and stamping—came from the Coard brothers. George and Arthur lived in the bungalow in Ma Coard's house.

Carnival, back then, created a spirit and carried the scent of paint used to print Angel Harps T-shirts for the steelband, the costumed sailor, and other presentations of the community's mas' bands. These tasks and more were entrusted to the talented Coard brothers.

In the bungalow, mop sticks, sneakers and other paraphernalia were decorated and customized to bring "fancy" into "Fancy Mas." The Bungalow was the place where George and Arthur transformed innocent men and women into "barbarians." The "privates" of the armed forces became "officers" during carnival celebrations. Steelband's men, outside of carnival, were assigned the roles of political advocates with their Pan-African and Black Power T-shirts.

All is not lost; there remains a reminder of the renowned creativity of the bungalow. Andre Garvey and Associates maintains a presence at the entrance of "Carnival Bungalow."

Andre Garvey picks up where George and Arthur Coard left off

Carnival Bungalow.

George Coard, artist and mas' man

Photo credit: Clarence Medford

Mas' In Yu Mas'

GEORGE COARD, WILLAN "Dupp" Dewsbury, Arthur Ramsay, John Bruno, Ken Sylvester, Robert Patterson, Dennis "Away" Lindsay, Derrick "Fatty Derrick" Clouden, Daisy Commissiong, and Francis Redhead are just a few who made valuable contributions to Grenada Carnival. These people can be labeled as "real mas' men and women." Let us never forget them.

It is extremely critical to remind ourselves of what was—not for the purpose of trying to remain relevant—but as a matter of optimism. The hope is that these constant reminders would force the conscience of the "masked men" (not mas' men) back to reality to drive their creativity. Thus, they'll avoid following the route of "easyism" and "skimpyism" to please the eyes of probers—with hardly a concern at satisfying the enthusiasm of those who crave a return of "real mas."

Masquerades of the past — "real mas"—comprising costumes stitched to perfection, by the nimble fingers of seamstress and tailors, were a competition in itself. With the exception of borrowed ideas and examples set forth by the greats in Trinidad and Tobago, the mere thought of the importation of costumes would have signaled an admission of failure by our mas' men and women. With them, creativity married pride—and supporters kept that relationship healthy.

Neighborhood participation ensured that when the shell blew, it was just to add some finishing touches to carnival preparations, including making the costumes. We will never be able to appreciate mas'—and make Grenada Carnival an envy once again—unless we look back at the men and women who sacrificed their time and money for the love of culture and the fringed benefits of enjoyment. Credit goes to the many who kept and shared these forgotten photos of "real people" and "real mas."

Arthur "Pumpkin Beard" Coard - Photo credit: Clarence Medford

Mas' Men

Willan Dewsbury, John Bruno, Robert Patterson.
MIDDLE George Coard, Skyie Redhead, and Richardo "Ricky" Keens-Douglas.
BOTTOM Winston "Tan Tan" Julien, Wilbur "Willie B" Thomas, and Peter Bain.

LONG BEFORE THE Monday and Tuesday street parades—and before the Monday-night mas' invasion was introduced—the anticipation, expectancy, and joy of carnival were created at the makeshift mas camps. It was an experience, and the exhilaration produced a healthy, contagious virus inside your body that was capable of destroying the cells of anxiety and pent-up frustrations.

This anticipation of carnival had side effects, and one was the urge to chip-chip—and not wine. As patrons crisscrossed the improvised mas' camps, a common thread was the pleasantries they exhibited. Ever present was the binder and sense of camaraderie that only a "true masquerader" can relate to.

The simple feat of choosing a section was a silent rivalry; it was understood by all but never spoken. It was an unspoken contest among mas' players, and they seemed to be saying, "We go see who look better on carnival day." That was "mas' of class"—"play mas" as Herby would utter in his sing-tone of voice.

Richardo "Ricky" Keens-Douglas.

We Played Real Mas'

"Land of the Pharaoh" (Rawle Steele).

Band of the Year winner: Derrick Clouden's
"Greek Mythology (Arthur Hosten).

Real Mas' (Herby).

Angel Harps on the road (George "Malaki" Johnson).
Below: Barbarians (George "Malaki" Johnson).

Angel Harps on Market Hill in 1961 Market Hill
and John Bruno's "Sailors Ashore

Pics compliment: George "Malaki" Johnson

Pics compliment: George "Malaki" Johnson

Pics compliment: George "Malaki" Johnson

Pics compliment: George "Malaki" Johnson

Diehard Supporters: No Pan Was Left Behind

ANGEL HARPS NEVER could've been the "people's band" without the contributions of its supporters. They came from various backgrounds and backyards. Community support was the glue that kept the band and the Wharf together through thick and thin and in good times and bad.

In victory and in defeat, supporters—men and women of the Wharf—stood by their band and defended it. It was firm and passionate backing that only political parties enjoy—without the band having to buy supporters. The loyalty of supporters was felt in the panhouse and on the road and on the stage and off the stage.

These supporters never gave others the benefit of thinking they were better than, or superior to, the Harps in competition. They were diehards and, perhaps, insanely fanatic. For them, it was Harps or nothing. When Angel Harps won on the judges' scoresheet, the band won in their hearts. And when the band lost on the scoresheet, the supporters still regarded the steel orchestra as their champions in every respect.

Among our supporters, however, some individuals and families must be singled out for special recognition. They're deserving of being listed and recorded in the parchment of the Angel Harps archives and history books.

There are many such distinguished supporters, but a few I need to mention are Skipper Bruce (Bruce Bain), Walter St. John, Baby (Rosalind Greenidge), Snooks (Winston Scipio), Pat Emmanuel, Titta/Mother B (Wilma Brathwaite), Ponty

(Michael Archibald), Brian Pitt, Lew Smith, Thomas Family, the La Hee family, the Cyrus family, the Coard family, the Steele family, the Maitland family, and the dockworkers of St. George's Port.

Tribute and commendation also must be paid to the parents who continue to be a pillar and a backbone to Angel Harps Steel Orchestra.

Walter St. John, Michael "Ponty" Archibald, Brian Pitt, and Lew Smith.

Bruce "Skipper" Bain. Winston "Snooks" Scipio.

In Maitland's Garage, pan stands were welded and prepared for the road.

Angel Harps Boycotted Mas'

IN 72 THE VIEUX COUR RECEICED A LICKING WHAT WERE THEY THINKING?

Leornard "Iggies" Noel

THE BEAUTIFUL, SUNNY Tuesday afternoon was full of sweet pan and masquerade. Harps had a playlist of some well-rehearsed tunes for the road. Our mas' band was the biggest we had seen in years, and the decision was made to split Harps into two sections to supply music for the masqueraders. I vividly remember playing in the second half of the band, directly behind the rhythm section, which was also fondly referred to as the "Engine Room".

We felt highly satisfied that, through our music performance, we were meeting the expectations of the revelers. They paid their fee of one dollar to jump with Angel Harps. They, not missing a beat, chipped and rocked from side to side to Sparrow's "Drunk and Disorderly" as we stopped on Granby's Street. "Drunk and Disorderly" won the Road March of Trinidad and Tobago in 1972.

I can't be sure if, from the Carenage where we started, we came over Market Hill or through the Sendall Tunnel to get into town, but the front of the mas' band was already positioned next to Y De Lima's Store, close to the old health center building, and where Andall's is now located. Without warning, those of us at the back of the band witnessed people frantically running toward us. The senior guys in Angel Harp began running toward the unknown disturbance. As they ran, they clutched steel pipes, iron, and chains—anything that could have been used as a weapon.

Members of Angel Harps, at the time, were not the type to shy away from a fight. They were hardened and seasoned soldiers, and they were ready to fight back at the slightest provocation. Sylvan, Ming, Smasher, Little Tom, and the Milkson brothers (Fatman and Bakay) were not the kind of people to mess with.

On that fateful Tuesday afternoon, someone from the crowded mas band shouted that Vieux Cour had tried to run through the band. What were these Vieux Cour thinking? They carried out an incursion into the wrong band, and they chose the wrong time to do it.

I reckoned the situation was grave when we were instructed to unload our pans and turn back toward the Wharf. That day is remembered as a day of carnage for the Vieux Cour. Those who came to disrupt our band left battered, bruised, and bloodied. A few of the pannists of Harps were students at St. John's Christian Secondary School (Schaper School). Immediately following the incident, they and their families agreed not to venture into Gouyave—where the Vieux Cour were based—and they sought and received transfers to other schools. To this day, I still wonder what the Vieux Cour masqueraders were thinking.

Commancheros and Associates (Rawle Steele).

Pictorial Interlude

Clarkes Court Pan Lovers, Guinness City Symphony, Angel Harps, Commancheros, Grand Roy Pan Angels—Rainbow City All Stars—Florida All Stars—New Dimensions—Pan Wizards.

Timmy Mason and the boys

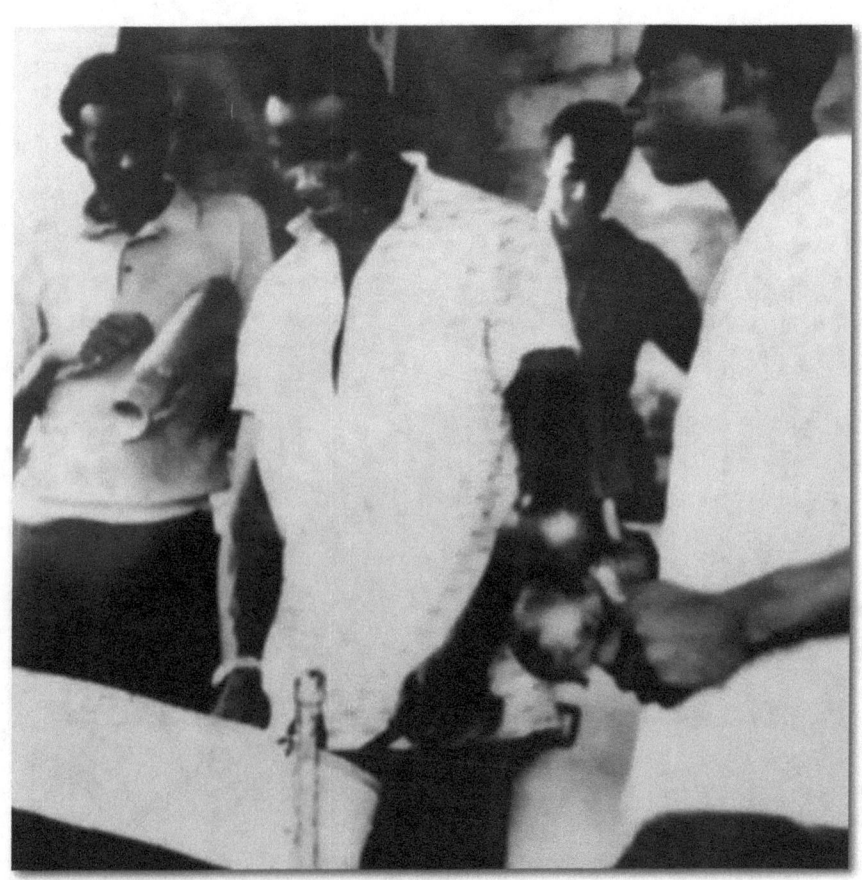
Terry "Gun" Lucas, Burk Drayton (middle) and Tony "Poo" Mitchell

Willian Dewsbury

Albert "Bert" Marryshow

Dunbar Steele

Wilfred "Sauce" Lewis

Mosley Parks

George Croney

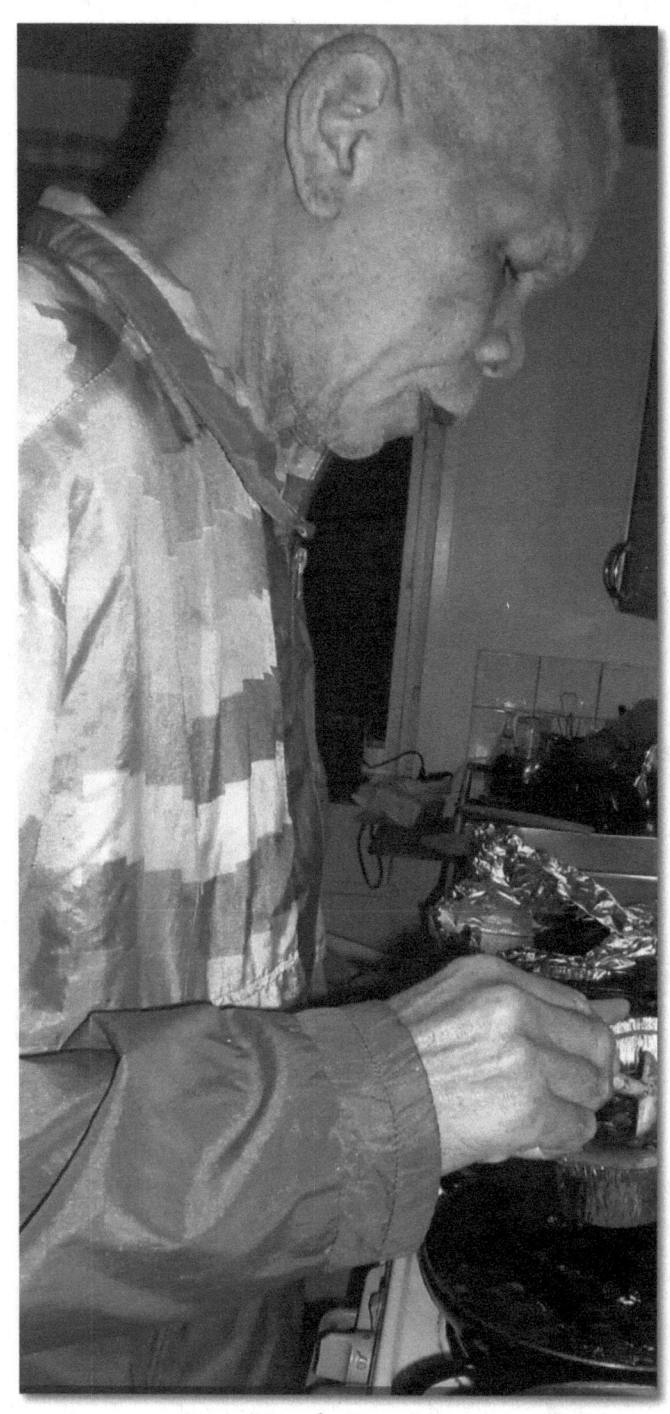

Steve "Spanky Bapp" Cyrus

Maestro: Lester Boyke

Charles Moses

"Will"

Wilfred "Harro" Harris

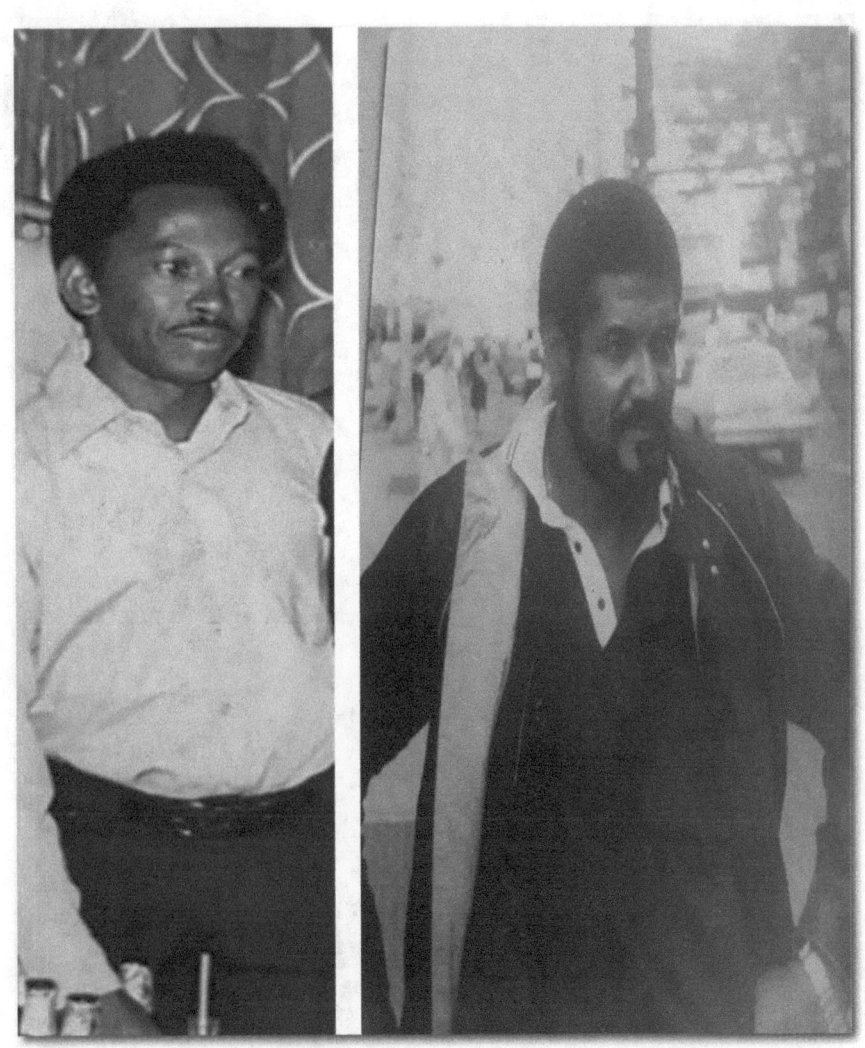
Dennis Phillip Evelyn "Bratt" Bullen

Joslyn "Jawbone" Felix

Arthur Coard

Robert Cadet

Trevor Emmanuel

Kenneth "Tiloti" Hood   David "Peck" Edwards

Cecil Noel

Guinness City Symphony

Guinness City Symphony

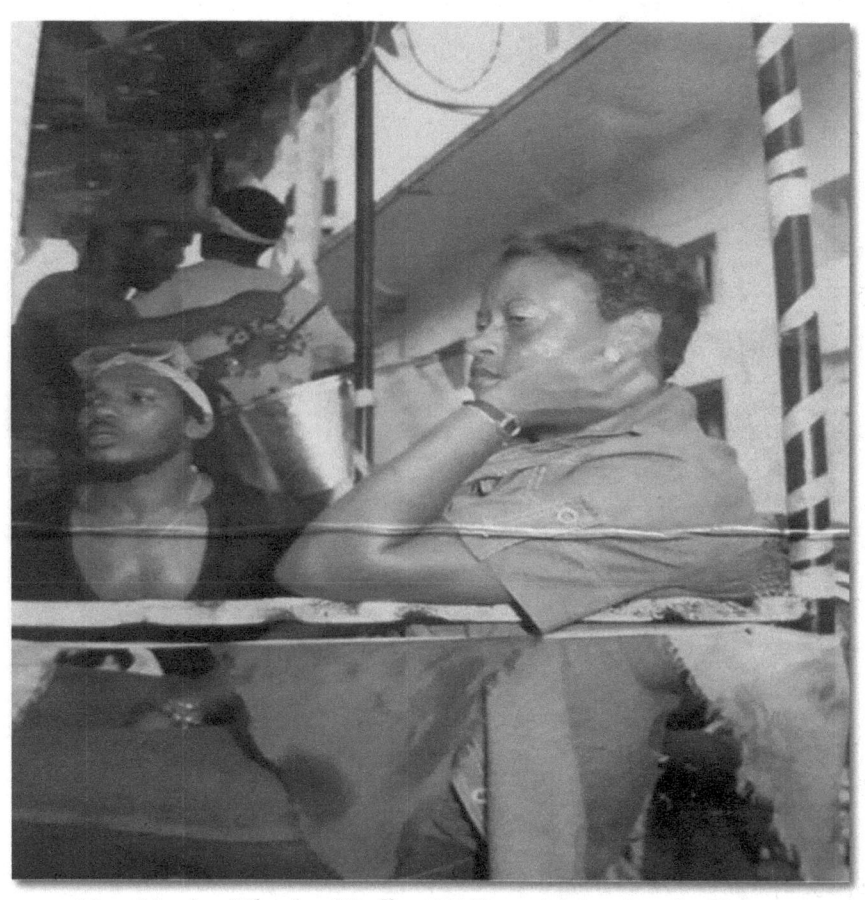

Mrs. Monica "Fletcher" Bullen: Riding with her band—Cheros

Mr. Smith as the pilot

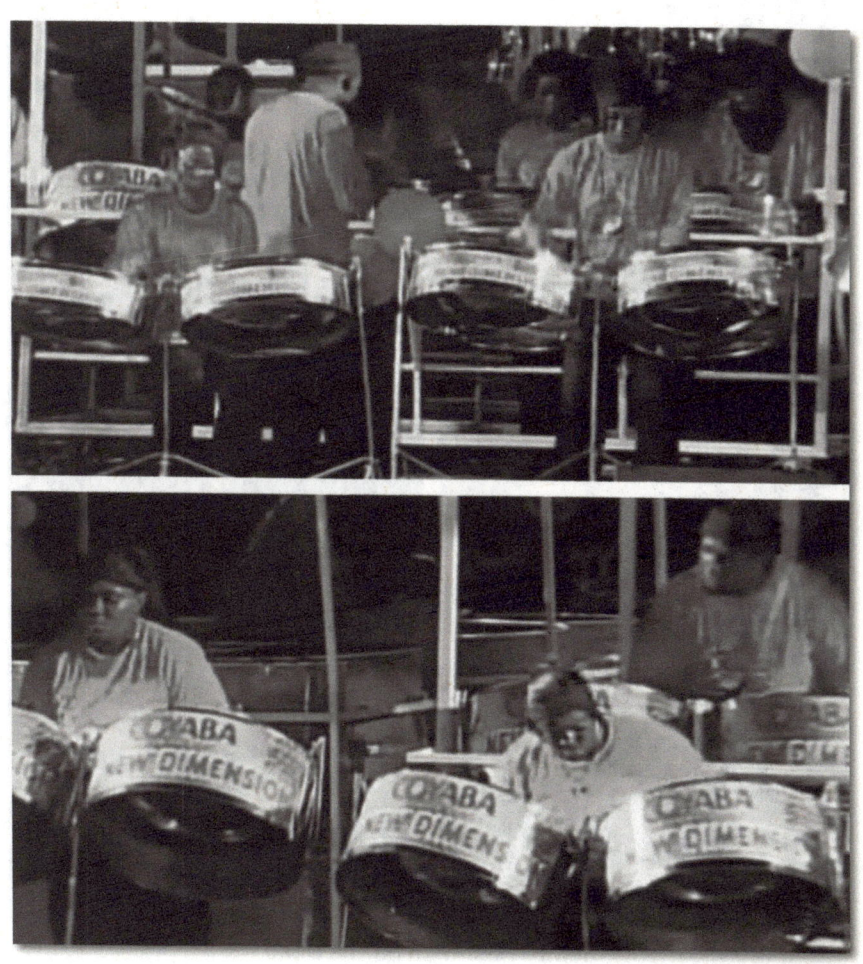
Coyaba New Dimensions

Before DJs—Pan on the Road

Pan Ossia

Pan Lovers

Florida All Stars

Melody Makers

Pan Wizards

Panorama Night

All eyes on the Pan

Ronald "Mitchie" Bain

Left to Right: Derrick, Merry and Depo

"South Stars" on Granby Street

Rejuvenated: South Stars Steel Orchestra

Top photo: With Mykal Blaize Robertson (Pan Wizards)—Below: Nigel Byam (New Dimension) and Kenton "Fry" Roberts

Commancheros on the Road

Angel Harps: Athletic Games Queens Park

Angel Harps: (2015) Celebrating their fiftieth anniversary

Rupert Glean: None Came Close

GRENADA IS KNOWN for its drama and theatrics and its scenery and scenes. However, if afforded a space at any one of the Madame Tussauds museums across the world and asked to submit a wax profile of choice, I'm sure Theophilus Albert (T. A.) Marryshow CBE, sometimes known as "Teddy" or "Albert," father of the West Indies Federation, would be a likely candidate. Other favorites are Sir Eric Matthew Gairy PC, father of independence and Maurice Rupert Bishop, prime minister of the People's Revolutionary Government and the leader of New Jewel Movement.

Outside of these renowned politicians, there is one person who contributed to the sphere of culture, particularly mas', that many who are under the age of fifty have probably never heard about. Rupert Alexander Glean was born in Grenada on July 30, 1930, and he passed away on April 2, 2020.

Rupert's creativity and versatility as a masquerader separated him from others, especially in the category of "Individual Portrayals." He was in a class of his own—competing against himself and vying for perfection against himself.

Rupert Glean won each year he entered into competition. Often, his depictions left many questioning whether what they were looking at was real or a replica. He created his own costumes and received acclaimed recognition for winning fifteen years straight. Some of Rupert's admired portrayals included Abraham Lincoln, Napoleon Bonaparte, Prince Philip, Sir Walter Raleigh, T. A. Marryshow, and Eric Gairy.

After his retirement and migration to North America, Grenada never again saw an individual masquerade performer like Rupert Alexander Glean. He took his love of the arts abroad, and his memorials are nowhere to be found in Grenada. Our loss. Rupert deserves a space in our yet-to-be-established "National Museum of Arts."

Rupert Glean portrayal of T.A. Marryshow, Michael "Smico" Marryshow)

Huge Apache Band (Queen's Park) making way
for Rupert Glean's individual portrayal.

What Carnival Come To?

Photos: Adrian Cummings and George "Malaki" Johnson.

THERE WAS A time when Grenada ranked second to Trinidad when it came to carnival and masquerade. Jab Jab had a mystical intrigue, and Shortknee, Wild Indian, and May Pole were unique to Grenada. Our costume displays were homegrown; the wire-bending and signature design pieces were produced by masters of the art form and were wildly admired. The masters were men such as Willan Dewsbury or "Dup Dup"—a nickname given to him as a pioneer of the steelpan sound. He was a contemporary of Trinidad pan pioneer Winston "Spree" Simon.

Masquerade production and display in Grenada evolved through the passion and creativity of others, including Primus from Belmont; Daisy Commissiong (first female contender from the Wharf), Dudley Hood and Dennis "Away" Lindsay from Green Street, the Coard brothers – George and Arthur from the Wharf. Other contributions came from Gordon Ramsay, John Bruno, and Ken Sylvester. They were followed by Robert and Dorothy Paterson, Derrick Clouden, Winston "Tan Tan" Julien, Waterman, Skyie Redhead, Pamela Douglas, and Wilbur Thomas—just to name a few. They made valid contributions to "real mas'."

Masquerade competition among these stalwarts was fierce, but it was amicable! The undertone was never money—just the love of carnival and fun. Back then, the focus was on various categories of competition such as "Individual Mas'," "Traditional," "Fancy," and "Historical." Rupert Glean was "untouchable."

I have yet to see anything remotely close to the bands of the past: The French Revolution, Apaches, Rom, To Hell and Back, Flag Wavers, Barbarians, Splendor of Egypt, Africa, and Quo Vadis. Sailor mas bands depicted masqueraders displaying ranks from private to lieutenants. Well-crafted floats that boggled the eyes often accompanied the officers.

Among the bandleaders from the Wharf/Green Street area were Daisy, George Coard, Ken Sylvester, and Away. Their rival bandleaders included John Bruno from "Town."

Every band had a faithful masquerader who was sure to play with you, year in and year out. That person, to the Wharf Band, was "Julie Pac Pac." She loved her mas', especially sailor depictions, and ranked herself high. She had one problem though; her anxiety about playing mas got the better of her. The band was scheduled to leave from in front of Empire Cinema at one thirty, and Julie Pac Pac would dress at nine o'clock, betraying what was supposed to be a secret until the start of masquerading in the afternoon. Nobody wanted to be in Julie's section.

Today, we hear the saying, "Is so we dey?" I ask, though, "What carnival come to?"

First female Band Leader from the Wharf: Daisy Commissiong (Photo credit: Richard Holstien)

Theophilus "Papitette" Redhead playing mas' (Photo credit: Pan Wizards)

First Dark-Skinned Carnival Queens

CARNIVAL WAS KNOWN for its splendor, beauty, and pageantry. The portrayals of kings and queens, villains and heroes, and adaptations of classic movies played out, with accuracy, on the streets of Grenada. From the reservations of "Flying Cloud" to the ridges of Africa; from "Davey Crocket" and to "Hell and Back" and the "French Revolution" and "The Glory of Rome," nothing was off limits for the creative minds of these mas'artisians.

The connotation of "bacchanal" was often relegated to the occasional clashes of steelbands, but that was few and far between. Jab Jabs were authentic masqueraders who showcased their mystique on Jourvert (Jouvay) morning, with boundaries not dictated by law but by conscience. Today, what we call Jab Jab is simply "Dirty Mas'."

In the case of Old Mas', it was advocacy for change and bringing hidden secrets to light through humor. The traditional Shortknee, Wild Indian, and Maypole dancers added an aura of genuineness. This, we cannot say, is any longer a feature or an element we can look forward to.

Outside of the street parades, the events leading up to carnival were tightly controlled and, I reluctantly admit, less cantankerous. Lord Melody, for example, operated the Calypso Tent in the Drill Yard on Young Street, and that was his. The Jaycees controlled the Queen Show.

The Carnival Queens contest brought out the "hifalutin of society," both as show participants and attendees. Sadly, the criteria laid out (not written, though) to be a contestant back then required the right pigmentation and "pedigree," before a young lady would even be considered—far more to receive commercial sponsorship—to be a Carnival Queen participant.

The barrier, the partition, that veil of prejudice was removed and broken down in 1963. It was the year a black, beautiful, bodacious, bedazzling young lady by the name of Florine Hope stepped on the Carnival Queen show stage. Florine blew past the ignorance of color prejudice with her intellect, charm, beauty, and aesthetics to capture the coveted crown—to the consternation of a few but the appreciation of many. Florine paved the way for a young Merril Ottley. Capturing the title years later, she endured less scrutiny for her skin color, but she also delivered another blow to the unwritten pigmentation qualification criterion for would-be contestants.

Salute to Florine Hope for her courage and small—but impactful—contribution in smashing the color ceiling in the Carnival Queen show in Grenada.

Florine Hope, Merril Ottley, and Noreen DeLeon on Green Street (Richardo "Ricky" Keens-Douglas).

Florine Hope and Merril Ottley (Word Press).

The Lime

My brothers Alister (Yankeyman) and Eric, Ben DeCoteau,

Milkson (Fatman), Claudius (Nose), Gerard (Daffy) and Katim Morgan on the Wharf.

"LIMING" HAS ALWAYS been with us and a part of us; the extracurricular activity enhanced our growth and exposed us to conversations, opinions, gossip, and fables with gravy. To the uninitiated, it seemingly was mere idleness, but it was a gathering with a purpose—squeezed tightly with juice and substance.

Age and circumstances determined our liming spots. An area carved out for liming were above Ms. Scott's house on Tyrrel Street. At times, she would threaten to call the police to stop us from "making noise" in her head, but she never did. We also went liming in and around Angel Harp's panhouse; Mr. Bridgeman's verandah, and on the steps separating the homes in the "bungalow," which was where the Bridgeman's and Belgrave's resided.

However, the Wharf proper—the bustling, humming seaside road strip—was the place where experience came nicely packaged, and our testosterone levels competed with the high tides of the inner harbor. Liming, for us, was productive, purposeful, and poignant. Liming was essential to our social upbringing and development and served us positively later in life, especially when leaving Grenada for foreign lands.

The memories and excitement of our limes are indelibly stamped on our minds. One of the most memorable night limes involved a few of us, including Richie, Orlando, Maga, and myself. We assembled at our second liming spot; above the bungalow, an area carved out for us close to Ms. Scott's house on Tyrrel Street. It was about 10:50 PM, Maga decided head for his home.

Maga was always the first to leave the group of limers; his journey home compelled him to pass in front of the house belonging to a man we called "Ligaroo Dolphus."

Ten minutes after taking leave of our group, we were shocked to see Maga sprinting back toward us, huffing and puffing and out of breath.

Out of deep concern for our friend and liming partner, we asked, "Wa happen, Maga?"

He replied, in a trembling voice, "A tall woman, dressed all in black, just stopped me to say good night, and I was unable to see her face."

Kirani James may have gotten the gold and silver at the Olympics, but after Maga relayed his encounter with the tall woman in black, our sprint relay team that night wasn't waiting for either one of us to pass the baton. The race was on in a desperate scamper to get home as quickly as possible. Where—or with whom—did Maga spend that night with? You will have to ask him when you see him.

Bertrand, Richie, Maga, myself, Andy, and Daffy.

Chinatown

LONG BEFORE UNCLE Gairy conceived the idea of Expo 69, his roving mind, vision, and insight brought Asia to us in the form of "Chinatown." This concept could not have come from the mind of a simpleton.

At the height of movies such as *The Sword Masters of Sienna,* *The One-Armed Swordsman,* and *Crouching Tiger, Hidden Dragon,* Gairy decided on Chinatown, locating it adjacent to the main entrance to the St, George's Pier. Uncle did not need approval from the cabinet for such a project, the blessings of the Conference of Churches, or the influence of public opinion to proceed. Imagine such daring by a politician today. Three people we knew came closest in resemblance to Chinese nationals: Ching from town, Chinaman from River Road, and Peter Boyke from the Wharf.

The Chinatown booths were manned by folks like Mamma, Ms. Bowen, and Mr. Shoot. Chinatown was the launching pad for those of us "looking for a head" before taking off to party at Hamilton Inn, Lion's Den, Pyramid, BBC, or Clancy Island.

Chinatown's "Ladies of the Night" were ever present to console those in need of comfort and commissaries. Mamma's booth was a favorite, especially when Cleopatra (Mamma's daughter) was behind the counter. She was a beautiful young woman, dark in complexion, and carried herself as an African princess to the envy of others.

Jimmy Cliff's reggae songs, popular in Chinatown, penetrated the surrounding areas of Tanteen and the Docks, and we eagerly searched for the intoxicated "head" by sipping on rum and cokes. The alcohol mixture lifted the spirits of the shy and anxious. Chinatown's fame was captured in a calypso by the same name. It was sung by a late police officer known by the stage name "Offkey."

Harold Pysadee, a Radio Free Grenada broadcaster at the time the calypso was released, sang the chorus of Offkey's "Chinatown" to me recently:

Chinatown was like Radio Free,
Keep you in touch with the news daily.
Anytime you go dey and hang,
You must see dem thief and hooligan.
A love Chinatown,
Chinatown.

Chinatown booth.

Rock Gardens, overlooking Tanteen with a view of the Docks and Chinatown.

Redevelopment of the area after Chinatown was demolished.

Petrolina: The Girls, Can-Can, and Sailors

WHEN MAN-OF-WAR SHIPS came into port and docked at the pier in St. George's, young boys such as Rex, "King Patch," and others would devise ways of evading the guards stationed at the port's front gates and find the galley to the American and British armored naval carriers. They had a unique style of communicating with the visiting sailors.

"Hey, Joe. Can you spare me something?" They would gesture toward their mouths.

The nights on the Wharf, Chinatown, and other areas in that vicinity, belonged to Petrolina, Muffin, Cutlass Foot, Pants Margaret, Joan, and Madame Jean. He, Madame Jean, was best known for his stenciled eyebrow pencil marks reaching his cheekbones. Madame Jean walked on his toes with his narrow backside swishing from side to side—as a Cooley Kite with bedding tail. The signature piece of Petrolina—or Petro—was her "Can-Can" and "high heels."

Muffin, even though her mouth was permanently fixed in a "strupsing" position, and "Cutlass foot," who walked as if she stole the "K" from the alphabet, were still able to attract a few boozehound sailors to rake in a few dollars at times; validating the old adage that "all stink cheese ha dey bread."

Of all the nightingales, one young lady by the name of Joan stood out. She carried herself as an Arabian mare, with class and elegance. Her presence always attracted our attention as we engaged in reckless eyeballing. And though we said little one to another about Joan, we all knew our antennas were tuned to the same frequency. The table was prepared for a banquet, yet the crumbs that fell beneath were still out of reach.

"Muffin."

Returning to a familiar spot on the Wharf with Richie, Bertrand, and Malu.

Prince Austin's First Visit to the Spice

WHEN MY GRANDSON, "Prince" Austin, left New York and landed on the Wharf for the first time, he met some real Wharf people. On the Wharf, Paupa and others sat and laughed at Grubay's hilarious tall tales. Stories were told for years before Ivan demolished Grubay's house at the entrance of the bungalow.

Prince Austin arrived at the place where Ms. Baby took ten minutes to serve you a hard three-cent cake and a Red Spot soft drink. On this very spot, John Parks would stop on his Humber bike to perform a salute and tell us about his war experiences. Leon headed in the direction of the pier, light as a feather, only to return an hour later, swiftly skipping by and thirty pounds heavier.

Prince Austin met real Wharf people at the place where Mafu, a deceased Angel Harps iron man, carried his rum glass—called an "eighths"—put the glass on the sidewalk, and conducted soliloquies like someone in a relationship with another person.

Prince Austin learned a lot, but there is so much more he has to learn about us Wharf people.

Prince Austin and his sister Alayna met Wharf people.

The Spout

THE SPOUT OFFERED a mini beachfront for bathing and an opportunity for boys to acquire their badge of honor as swimmers. Being labeled as a "nonswimmer" back then invited ridicule and teasing.

On early mornings, it was not unusual to witness grown men making their way to the Spout with bunches of "Cooly Pawpaw" bush in their hands. The bush was a substitute for soap.

The Spout also served as a temporary shelter to fishermen, particularly those from St. Vincent. Many of the Vincentians, after considerations and afterthoughts, took up residency and established families in Grenada. The Spout was located just off to what is now the headquarters of the Public Workers' Union headquarters in Tanteen, directly beneath the yacht club. With no road to the Spout, a track was created to gain access. Getting there—maneuvering between picker trees to your right and left—required skills.

Immediately above the trail was the GBSS barracks and a hostel for boys. Tutelage of the hostel boys was entrusted to the authoritarian, Ms. Brathwaite, and her roaming eyes. The hostel was a place where proper etiquette, decorum, and manners were imparted to its occupants.

Parents often warned children to avoid visiting the Spout whenever a boat was scheduled to be launched. Why? The answer resided in a superstition about launching boats and the devil. It was said that launching boats and Satan's requiring souls worked together.

Adjacent to the Spout, the south side of the
Grenada Yacht Club (Peter/Peterlyn).

Ms. Brathwaite, warden of the GBSS Hostel, directly above the Spout.

Inspector Hurley, James Lowe, and the Ganja Tree

THIS STORY CAME from the same source that relayed the event of Holly's transformation of the fellas from mas' band players to an "elite police squad" without going through basic training; this source, if I may say so, is very reliable and was an active participant—directly involved—in this story. Therefore, I feel somewhat comfortable in retelling it and saying, "So I buy it, so I will sell it—with no profit to this salesman."

In the sixties, in pre-Independence Grenada, Premier Eric Gairy decided to make the Police Band musicians work for their salaries. The decision was to incorporate the musicians into the standing police force; to many of the newly recruits, that decision was not music to their ears.

However, anyone who knew Uncle Gairy would understand how resolute he was. To those who frowned on his idea and decision, he said, "You all are police first and band men after." Even with the combined duties, he expected the same level of proficiency in music when Police Band members were summoned to perform at ceremonial functions. They had to be ready and prepared to play the role of top-class musicians.

Meanwhile, ganja was emerging as the new "thing" on the block. There was no shortage of cow grass, wheat grass, stinging nettles, and the real thing, ganja, in the scramble to experiment with getting a high from Mary Jane.

A few young men from the Wharf, on two occasions, found themselves smoking "something" in a house behind George Street. The smoky scent was so heavy that it couldn't be hidden, even with the pleasant aroma emanating from the nearby Lime Factory.

From among the Police Band members, four men were selected to participate in Royal Grenada Police Force training, which was being supervised by Inspector Arnold Hurley. Two of the four were recent Police Band conscripts. Training was in a little room at the fire station on the Wharf.

The focus of the training was on sight, smell, and symptoms—with the presence of a ganja tree to enhance teaching and learning. However, every day after training, someone would pull a leaf from the tree, hoping Inspector Hurley would not notice. One day, a trainee by the name of James Lowe—a Police Band member—decided he wanted two leaves instead of one. In his haste, he accidentally grabbed a branch and a half, holding it and standing right before Mr. Hurley.

Instead of bringing charges against James, the goodly senior officer—who later was promoted to assistant superintendent of police—recommended a punishment that included Lowe's paying off all the money he owed to the police canteen. Lowe also was given a six-month assignment to Carriacou and a year of physical training in Barbados. His friends never allowed James Lowe to rest, remembering him always as "Two Leaves and Low Branch" Lowe.

Lord Melody - Punks

TODAY, WE HAVE calypso "associations," "organizations" and "confusion." We also have soca monarch, groovy and kaiso competitions. Decades ago, it was one man, one calypso tent, and one association—and it all belonged to "Melody" or "Punks. His real name, given at birth, was Wilfred Baptiste.

His operational headquarters and show venue was the Drill Yard on Young Street. It was a very strategic location. If you think it is easier for a camel to pass through the eye of a needle than a rich man to enter heaven, trying to "scheme in" on Melody at the Drill Yard was even more daunting.

The cast at Melody's "Firestick Calypso Tent" included the likes of Scaramouche, Unlucky, Gospo, Pappitette, Stumpy, Dictator, Rouke, Darkie, Hurricane, and Slim. Mighty Lizard, who sang at the Firestick Tent too, often whipped up the audience with his off-key songs, leaving all and sundry rolling with laughter. Lizard had no qualms stopping the band at times to chastise the band's drummer, Redman, for not keeping in rhythm with him.

The Mighty Pirate debuted as a calypsonian at the Drill Yard; yes, our Pirate from the Wharf. His breakout song almost caused Ms. Nella to "bring him up." She threatened to file a lawsuit against the Mighty Pirate.

Every night at the Firestick Tent, the calypsonians gave the audience their fifty-cents' worth (the entrance fee to the Drill Yard was fifty cents). They were treated to memorable calypsoes such as "Commansingh," "Monica Karway," and "Brighter Out Of Darkness."

Melody was not just the chief organizer, general manager, chief cook, and bottle washer at the Firestick Calypso Tent; he also split his time doing other gigs. He was a hired voice heralding advertisements for businesses in St. George's. Whether it was a sale at L.A. Purcell, DeFreitas, Everybody's, or Noble Smith, he was their voice. Upcoming premier events at Empire or Regal Cinemas also were announced by Melody.

With his signature kerchief hanging from his back pocket and narrow-peak saga boy hat, Melody did not wait for business to come to him. He met it halfway and did what he had to do: singing calypso, spinning the wheel of Lucky 7, or bellowing over a bullhorn. Publicly broadcasting sales—for dresses, petticoats, bloomers and tablecloths—Melody (Punks) did what he had to do to make a shilling.

Information obtained from the Grenada National Trust/Angus Martin stated: "The Calypso tent in the Drill Yard was opened in 1958, where the likes of Lord Melody and Quo Vadis ushered in the modern era of Grenadian calypso. Bomber (Clifton Ryan) won the calypso king in Grenada between 1940 and 1947, and went on to win the crown in Trinidad in 1964."

Quo Vadis, Bomber, and Invader (Wikimedia, John Fredericks, and Angus Martin).

Other calypsonians from the Drill Yard tent:
Pappitette, Mighty Rouke, and Eagle.

Lord Slim.

Old Drill Yard and Melody's "Firestick" Calypso Tent.

Mr. Redman

THERE ARE SO many fond memories of people, including "Redman," who made an impression on us while growing up. When saluting him in public, he was addressed as "Mr. Redman." Like with Melody, Redman was not his name at baptism. However, Redman was what he was known by; it was the name by which most people knew him. It is what he was called and to which he answered. I suspect the "Redman" came about because of his golden crust complexion.

Ascribing a moniker to someone was not unusual. Most folks were known by one name only, and it was often an alias. Once bestowed on you, that nickname would outlive you.

Mr. Redman, to his family and on official documents, was Kyron Charles.

Redman was best known as a lawn tennis coach. He conducted sessions at the Tanteen Tennis Court for young people of all ages—credit Uncle Gairy for that. Tennis was Uncle's sport of choice, and cricket was a close second. I don't know if he settled on the choice of tennis and cricket because he looked angelic in white or if it was a statement of defiance to those, especially the tennis players of the day, who regarded tennis as a privileged sport for a certain class of people. Uncle may have been motivated by both considerations to participate in tennis and cricket.

Interestingly, Redman was also Uncle's coach and whipping boy when crowds gathered to witness his polished frame in motion on the courts. Unlike others, who used the names "Redman" and "Mr. Reds," Uncle referred to him as "Reds." He was the only person to address him in abbreviation.

On one occasion, Redman became a bit overambitious while knocking with Uncle. He began lobbing some fancy serves toward Uncle Gairy—only to be pulled aside and scolded. Uncle said, "Reds, we have spectators—and you are making me look bad."

I don't have to tell you what type of serves Uncle Gairy received after that.

In addition to coaching, Redman played drums for Solid Cinders (Wakax) band. It was a version of that band that played in the Drill Yard for Melody's "Firestick Calypso Tent."

Grenadian tennis star Akilah James on the court constructed by Uncle in Tanteen.

Uncle Paid Attention to His People: Emulations and Recognitions

Rupert "Big Bear" Willams

Credit: Anthony DeRiggs

Rupert "Big Bear" Williams
(Anthony DeRiggs)

RUPERT "BIG BEAR" Williams towered over many in physique and stature. He was a giant of a man with little tolerance for the wranglings of committees and organizations. He wasn't one to get tied up or bogged down with red tape. To avoid such encumbrances, he became his own one-man committee, accountable only to himself, in organizing the Tanteen Soft Shoe Football Competition in the sixties. No one asked about game fixtures, but one was provided at the beginning of every competition. No team inquired about field equipment and supplies, such as nets and balls, but they were in place every soccer season. Referees and linesmen were "touch and go," and when none was available to officiate, Big Bear became their substitute.

The Tanteen Soft Shoe Competition brought out the best talents during Grenada's supremacy in football. The Dazzlers, Bluerooms, Santos, Point, and Demons provided a spirit of competition and a fierceness that showcased some of the most talented players who went on to represent Grenada on the national team. Players, known or remembered mostly by nicknames, included Sampat, Mayor, Big Dog and Small Dog, Major Jackson, Sheepy, the LaCrette brothers, Spinny, Ram Folkes, Sonnell, Dracula, James Clarkson, Dan-da-Rat, Michael Cummings, and Finton Maitland.

El Tigre was never a serious competitor but offered spectators boundless entertainment. A majority of players comprised men who loved their grog. With Piggy and Cressy as goalkeepers, we saw more staggering than diving within the restricted lines of the goalpost. Inebriation! Rupert "Big Bear" Williams singlehandedly made this happen. To him, we say, "Thank you!"

Bear had a passion for football, and that was further demonstrated in his assistance—from his personal resources—to primary and secondary schools that participated in the Junior League Competition.

: Fitzpatrick "Sheepy" Belgrave (Sheepy and Michael Cummings).

Dazzlers Football Team

Rawle Steele.

Charlie Hood: Old Trafford and Carenage United

Charlie (sitting in Old Trafford) reflecting on the past.

DURING THE SEVENTIES, Charlie Hood picked up the dimmed torch from Rupert "Big Bear" Williams. Charlie, with the help of others from the Carenage and Tanteen, pulled together teams of players from the community to showcase their talent at the famous Old Trafford Football Competition.

Like Bear's Soft Shoe Competition, Old Trafford soccer became a marquee event with a compelling force—enough to bring the Grenada Football Association (GFA) to its knees. It evolved into an annual sporting spectacle with class; it was rich in uniformity, territorial in support, and rewarding for those who came out on top as winners. And, though the playing field did not meet the regulated standards, it did not diminish the caliber of games at Tanteen's Old Trafford.

Teams from every community vied for the championship trophy. Unlike the preceding Soft Shoe Competition, Old Trafford players were rewarded with medals and individual trinkets in recognition of their accomplishments. Formidable teams in the tournament included NJM United, Halifax City, Phoenix Third World, and Nahous Scrunters.

Traffic on the Tanteen main road came to a standstill whenever teams came up against one another. The Soft Shoe Competition had El Tigre, and Old Trafford had Rockshire. Team members of Rockshire was not known for being lovers of the 'spirits' as El Tigre players. Most teams saw them as an easy target for their point standings in the competition. Rockshire – led by the late Joe John and Alister "Big Baby" Gittens were the only two outsiders playing for the team. The majority of the players came from the Heywood family.

The irony of all this, was an encounter between Rockshire and Phoenix (a top contender in the competition). The game, before it started, was considered by most as "sure points" for Phoenix—until Rockshire pulled off the seemingly impossible. The team put a sound licking on Phoenix that afternoon; it's something I will never forget. The bullying of Rockshire was over. It's a victory, I'm sure, that surviving members of Rockshire have engraved on their walls.

Whether it was fluke or fake, the one thing we can all agree on is that it was a flogging of Phoenix. Before the commencement of the match, if anyone—former or current football fan—told me with a straight face that they believed Rockshire would have earned a consolation draw, much less a win, I would have thought they were crazy.

Over-forty competition on Old Trafford Ground (Cheney Joseph).

Charlie went on to be an integral part of Carenage United Sports Club in the GFA First Division and Premier League, fielding players such as Sack, Barry, Toro, Boyo, Yankeyman, Trevor, Fly, Barabbas, Richard, Rudolph, Bread, Piey, Boose, Gevoskie, Ulric, Guapo, and Shamrock.

Shocker: Police defeat Dano Carenage 5–2!

In Memorial: Dr. Winston Thomas

DR. WINSTON THOMAS, "Stan" and "Doc," as he was fondly called, was the epitome, the embodiment, and the personification of a selfless servant. He, coming from a humble upbringing of the Thomas family from George Street, was an authentic Wharf boy. His humility, gentility, and mannerisms far superseded his accomplishments as a medical doctor.

The "People's Doctor" was always accessible to offer his services to anyone and everyone without remittances from patients. Winston truly was a staple, an anchor, and a lifesaver within the community of the Wharf; this, by no means, is an exaggeration of who he was as an individual. As a servant and a doctor, Dr. Thomas truly is greatly missed. He defies the proverbial statement that "no man is indispensable." He was indispensable. His contributions and input in politics were also invaluable and always predicated on the principles he held and not on the individuals and party he supported. He was a standard-bearer for selflessness. Rest in peace, Doc.

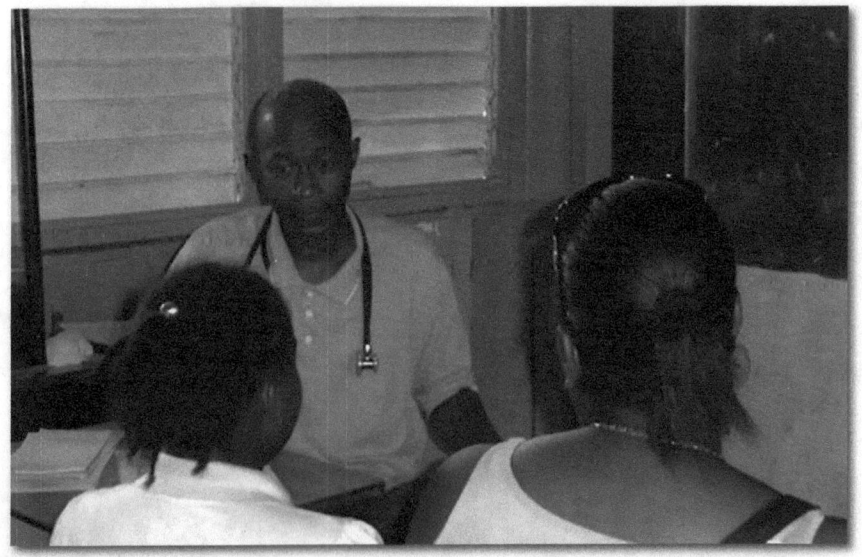

Dr. Thomas with his patients.

Panmen: In Memorial

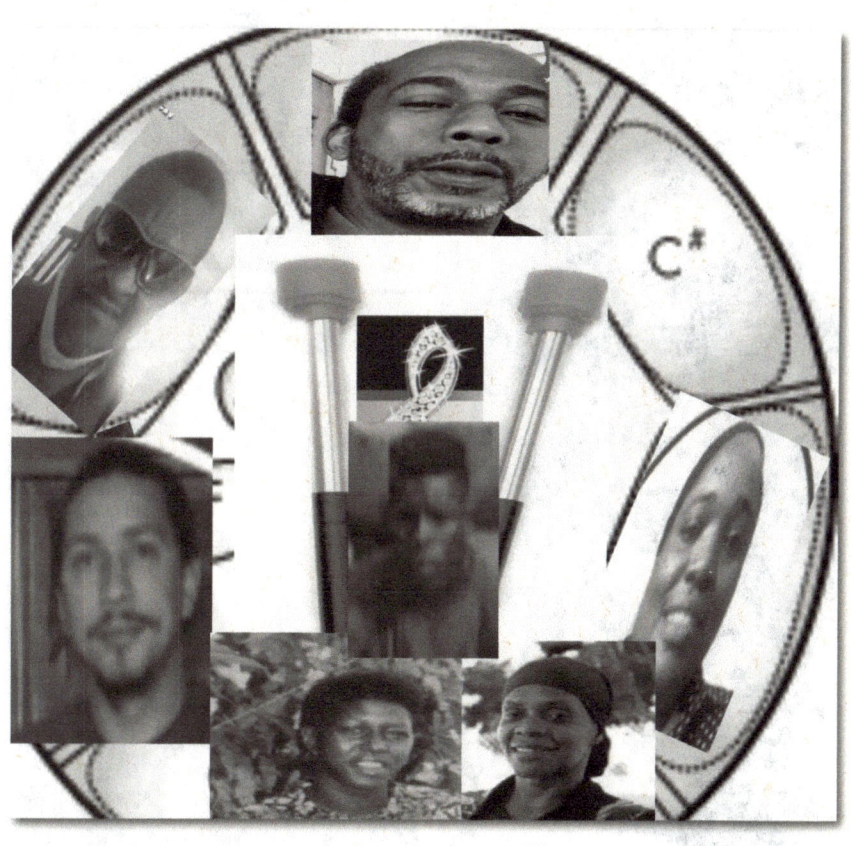

He Keeps the Wharf Clean

THEOPHILUS "TAFFY" STEPHEN is now his late eighties, and he has been a fixture on the Carenage/Wharf doing what he does best for most of his life, singlehandedly trying to keep the waters of this inner-locked harbor free from trash and debris. This is a task he has dedicated his life to. Despite his age, he still shows a determination to continue doing it not for pay but for pride. He is not one to engage in idle babblings, but if and when the conversation is centered around cleanliness, you can bet your life he will not hesitate to give his honest opinion on such.

"Taffy" is not bashful in crediting Sir Eric Matthew Gairy for keeping Grenada clean during his tenure. His admiration often points to the areas where this was evident, contrasting with what we see today both on land and in rivers and seas. In a recent interview with journalist Curlan Campbell, "Taffy" stated, "Years ago, since I know the Carenage, it was never dirty in the days of Mr. Gairy, but after his death everything changed and the Carenage is now a mess. It's a real sea perseverance" (dumping ground). He often laments the lack of respect from citizens and how callous they are today toward the natural environment—and about bus drivers and motorists who become enraged as he transports the refuge on the streets to a specific dumping site.

Though many pay little notice to him for his contribution, recently a Grenada Green Group Association hailed "Taffy" and recognized him as an unsung hero for the work he does. I too would like to say thank you to Mr. Theophilus "Taffy" Stephen.

Pictorial: The Sounds of Grenada in the Past

GRENADIAN BANDS INCLUDE Jahjah Children, Three Plus Two, Quavers Combo, The Weevils, Moss International, Magnificent Six, Blue Bird Combo, Harmonies with Brass, Caress, Pilgrimage with Brass, Ammonds 8, Melotone, Rhythm Riders, Fantasies, Harmony Kings, Paramount, Solid Senders, Maestros, United Rhythm, John Bo Boo Big Band, Mutineers, Teenage Thrillers, Luv Sound, Black Experience, and Scottie and the Brass.

In the mid-1960s and early 70s, talent was truly afloat with brass bands and combo bands throughout the length and breadth of Grenada. Brass bands—the likes of Solid Cinders, Rhythm Riders, Maestros, Moss, and later Pilgrimage—energized patrons at dance parties and other events with their beautiful music.

However, in the musical mix, there emerged combos (many rooted by school affiliation, family ties, and common acquaintance through friendship), similar to those we followed from Liverpool to New Orleans. These youthful combo bands included Cardinals, Fantasies, Teenage Thrillers, Weevils, Inner Circle and Minstrels. They all held their own, but there was one exceptional band: Luv Sound!

Luv Sound elevated the music of that era to another notch. Their dedication and devotion to what they did came through in their music. Dancing or listening to Luv Sound was a "LOVE SOUND" to enjoy.

Teenage Thrillers.

Maestros Orchestra.

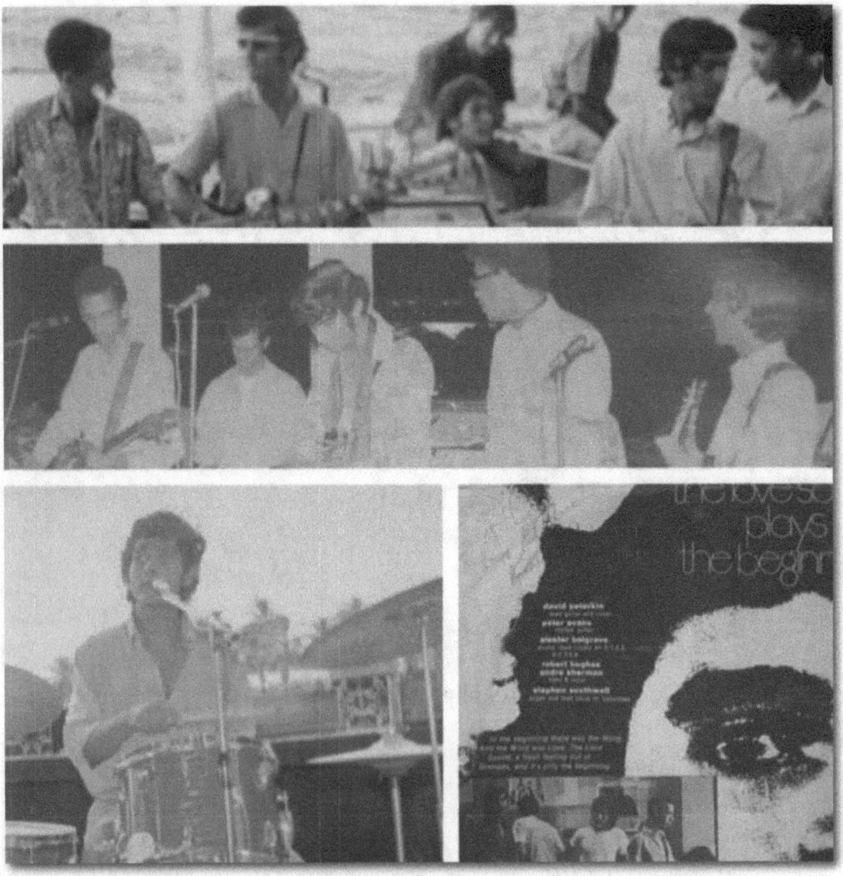

Luv Sound.

Mutineers

The Weevils.

Pilgrimage.

Moss International.

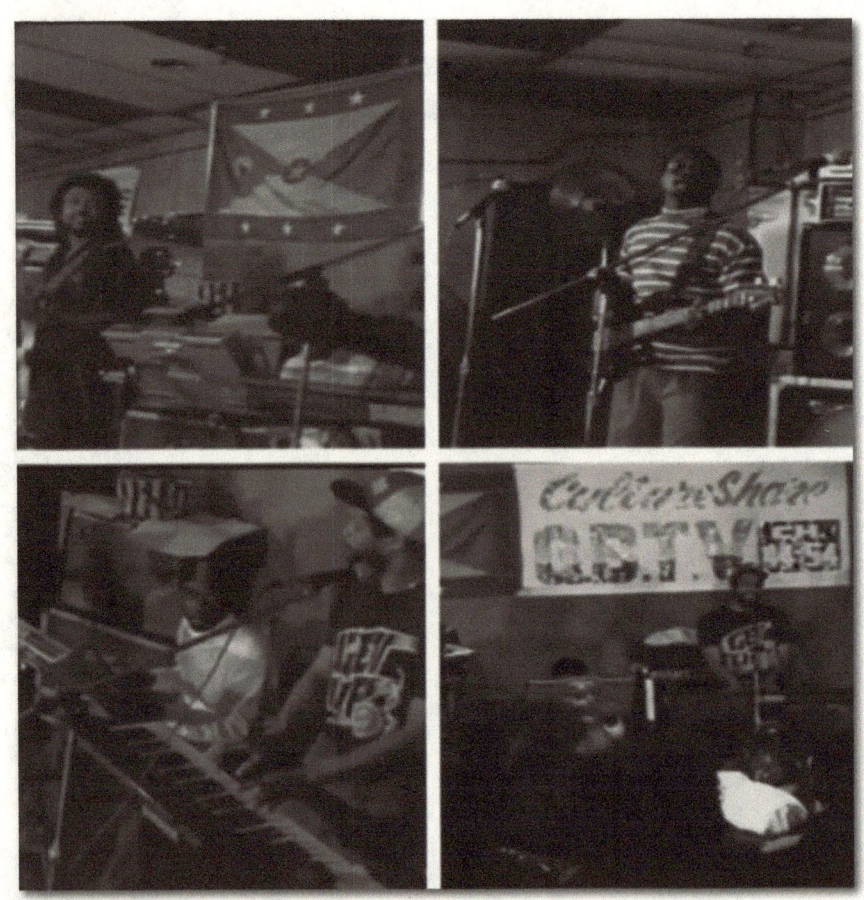

Oasis Band.

Jahjah Children.

Broko on his instrument

MANY YOUNGSTERS TODAY, and those below the age of fifty, have never heard of George Simon (Broko). His nickname was given because of his obvious leg impediment. Unlike others, he was never offended by the sobriquet given to him. George Simon may have been on his birth certificate, but "Broko" is the name by which Grenadians knew him.

As a musician, he was very versatile. His versatility and talent on the saxophone made him a giant among men in the late fifties, sixties, and early seventies at dance halls throughout Grenada.

There is a rare photo capturing "Broko" on sax and some elderly folks elegantly performing a few traditional dances. The photo is a reminder of the loss of many traditional dances to the strangulation of the indigenous and original in favor of the foreign and imported.

Youthful Teasing and Taunting

"IF YOU DON'T have good foot, take in front." That grassroots proverbial saying was always in the forefront of our mischievous minds, particularly when the target of our teasing and taunting was someone who was quick on his feet. Mr. Coard (Red Ants), who lived on Tyrrel Street, was an easy prey. He was always stationed at the front of his door, and we knew there was no need to run when we heckled him. What he did have though, was every expletive you can think of in his "curse book." He also had the unique premonition of targeting accurately (by name), one in the the group of young people teasing him. From behind his door, he would exclaim, "Coslyn Boy, ah hear you!" How he was able to pinpoint "Coslyn Boy" as Maga, we could not tell. "Sea Water Bread" was a brisk walker, but he lacked stamina; "Britain Donkey" was like the biblical David with stones; she pelted them with the exactness of a sharpshooter.

We deliberately avoided "One-Foot Sylvie" because of her constant threat to "work obeah" on us. The two people we most were afraid of taunting were "Tall Seppy" and "Stone Bruise."

Like Red Ants, Tall Seppy resided on Tyrrel and had once worked as a chauffeur for Premier Eric Matthew Gairy. Seppy kept a sharp cutlass at an arm's length. His six-feet-plus frame was also an intimidating factor. With Seppy, distance between him and us depended on whether to tease or not to tease. If you did not have "good foot," it was advisable to "take in front." The most athletic of them all were "Stone Bruise" and "Sergeant Doggie."

Stone Bruise was a tall man with hands like a stingray and feet like an ostrich. He occasionally slept in the boathouse—better known as "the Fisherman's Motel"—that was located in the Spout.

Teasing Stone Bruise came with risks; a slap from him had the potential of practically "outing your light." Stone Bruise, as well, possessed the speed of a hundred-meter runner and stamina enough for an eight-hundred marathons without breaking a sweat.

Sergeant Doggie showed up on the Wharf unexpectedly and soon became a fixture of the community. He, similar to Seppy and Stone Bruise, was particularly agile on his feet.

As boys on the Wharf, we embraced teasing and taunting. A risk or adventure, but a sport to us.

Window-Shopping: Liking What We Could Not Afford

AS CHILDREN, "WINDOW-SHOPPING" to us was just "window shopping." Nevertheless, we did not mind liking what we could not afford to buy. Our eyes were glued to Big Frenchie's, hoping by Christmas to have enough in our pockets to purchase a "pony gun." If we did not have enough to buy it, we would settle for the shots to pound with stones on the ground.

The Beauty of Christmas Eve

Yes, that was the beauty of Christmas,
Every house yu pass, yu cuda knock a glass.
With either ginger bear, sorrel, or strong rum
Punch-A-Cream with bay leaves, cinnamon, and nutmeg for flavor,
A slice of salt ham to keep yu sober,
And something on the run to carry you over.
The women stayed up late to bake bread and cake,
all with only two hands,
And still found time to reshuffle the house
Our parents were more than magicians
Yes! That was the beauty of Christmas
Window-shopping as children, we did two weeks before
Walking two and three times in front Amado store
Christmas Eve, as we got older, was our liberation day
No set time to come and go, it was our time to play
No longer scrambling to buy a "Chicken Snack" at Nutmeg Restaurant
That we were able to achieve
Why? Because we had cash in our pockets, on Christmas Eve

Nutmeg Bar and Restaurant.

Christmas Eve Was Special

CHRISTMAS WAS SPECIAL, but Christmas Eve was spectacular! Our parents allowed us to own the Eve, and children claimed it with a vengeance. Prior to that long-awaited day, we found a measure of satisfaction in stretching our imagination by "window-shopping." We were not being covetous, but we remained appreciative of the little we had. No complaints were uttered. We also walked past, very many times, the Esplanade Promenade (where the Esplanade Mall is now located), admiring the numerous gift boxes swinging provocatively from branches of the huge trees rooted there. The Esplanade then was a beautiful, reserved compound set aside for relaxation. By our teenage years, we no longer had change or coins making noise in our pockets; we now were carrying dollar bills. Dollars for chicken snacks, the movies, and packets of "Three Fives" cigarettes instead Royal and Phoenix. No longer was it necessary to "scheme" our way into dance parties; we paid to get in. Neither, anymore, did we buy our clothes from the Syrians in town; we secured our "threads" from Trinidad and selected the skillful mastery of tailors such as "Away," "Looky," "Tailor Man," and "Gums" to fashion our pants and shirts.

Charles of Grenada was the store where ordinary, poor, working-class folks peeked into from the outside. Only those with "pesh" in their wallets went inside to shop. It was from Charles of Grenada where we purchased our footwear, including authentic desert boots—straight from London.

Our parents, in making ends meet, were virtual year-round magicians, but especially so at Christmas. With extra vigor and enthusiasm, they transformed the entire house in the wink of an eye. Up to this day I have no idea how they did it, within a short space of time, but they did. Turning the house upside down, moving the Morris chair and the cabinet. The chairs, with plaited straw at the back, obtained from L. A. Purcell, shuffled around in a frenzy prior to Christmas day.

On Christmas morning, if the crowing of cocks did not wake you up, you were sure to rise from your slumber by the aroma coming through the kitchen window of the baking of bread, cake, ham with "chow-chow," and the scent of cocoa tea.

Christmas Then and Now

LET'S TALK ABOUT Christmas then and Christmas now. Christmas, at the time of my childhood, was synonymous with the smell of the linoleum and plastic fruits in a bowl on a table. The fruits looked real, but we knew it was not edible. I remember the tablecloths, purchased at Maria Scott, covered with attractive designs in preparation for Christmas. The Syrian storeowners stayed true to this proverb: "If you can't go to the mountain, the mountain can come to you." Their pricing, and with walking salesmen, allowed our parents to purchase commodities, such as terylene and gabardine fabric, from them. Central to our Christmas enjoyment was the anticipation of tasting the church wine during the Novena service. However, nothing was more rewarding than "window-shopping", particularly when broke! But all in all, we delighted in Christmas and never gave a second thought to the word "poor."

The Greasy (Ham) Pole

BOXING DAY AND New Year's Eve brought the daredevils out to see who can snatch one of the several hams attached to the tip of a "greasy pole" on the Wharf. Men and boys tried different techniques to keep their bodies from slipping off the poles. Hossay and Peter Boyke showed masterful dexterity as they twisted their frames with acrobatic maneuvers—flying in the air as Superman—to get the ham at the end of the greasy Pole. Yes, those lost indulgences offered fun and laughter.

The Revolution: Hope and Betrayal of Trust

IT IS FAIR to say when I migrated to the United States in the 1970s—on the heels of most of my friends—politics was the farthest thing from my mind. And although the seeds of black consciousness were already embedded in our psyches (to some extent), influenced by the trends of certain African Liberation Movements and Progressive Organizations worldwide, our main purpose migrating to the USA was to see how we could hitch a ride on that subway of prosperity; streets paved with gold, only to face the reality of decadence, and then realizing the American dream was more survival of the fittest under some very unkind weather conditions.

The opportunity for equalization that marginalized us in Grenada was no longer slanted, and it became a leveled playing field with many surprises. It wasn't about name, educational subjects obtained, family background, or complexion. We all had to learn how to maneuver to survive in that "concrete jungle." We left the Wharf, but we never forgot the Wharf—and that served us well.

Some worked in factories, and others worked in construction (always peeping and dodging). We looked forward to Saturday night when the pent-up aggravation of our weekly toils was released and exhumed like a form of exorcism in the well-known party halls around Brooklyn. We felt guilty at times when we saw church folks heading to their place of worship, and we were heading to a White Castle for breakfast.

A lot did change after 1979. When the revolution took place in Grenada. We began to cherish the simple things we had left behind for this utopian dream. Our grasp of the starlight in America seemed further than we had ever imagined. The promises of the Revo caught our attention and drove many of us to consider our lot as to how we would be able to contribute to that new idea, that new process. To do so, education became paramount in our conversations.

Some, without the required acumen of GCE (General Cambridge Examination) subjects (like myself), obtained our GED's (General Education Diploma), which was the minimum entry requirement to get into a college/university. Most of us began this next phase of our education attending the NYC Technical College (two year institution) and transferred to four-year CUNY institutions such as Baruch, Long Island University, Brooklyn College, and Polytechnic Institute.

Driven by enthusiasm, patriotism, and nationalism, the Grenada Revolutionary League (GRL) was formed and became the backbone, the watchtower, and the main defender of the Revolution in New York. GRL was the first organization in North America to purchase airport bonds when that project was embarked upon; at a time when the construction of the airport came under serious attack by the Reagan administration. Our fundraising efforts in support of the revolution and its programs, were not only seen as a patriotic gesture, but acknowledged and endorsed by the leadership of the PRG (People's Revolutionary Government).

Full confidence in GRL as an organization was unquestionable. Maurice Bishop's last appearance at Hunter's College in June 1983—to a standing-room-only audience—was a collaborative effort between the Consulate Office in New York and GRL. The demise of the PRG and the revolution in October 1983 became another wedge for me. I was in a hard place with little room to wiggle. The loss of lives and those who lost their livelihoods and families through the misguided program of isolation and detention without redress, had become a concern to us.

The collapse of that experiment left an indelible mark on us, considering the sacrifices made by many to realize the dream of "Forward Ever, Backward Never." We were in retreat. All was not lost though. The inspiration of the Revo bore fruit, and the motivation to continue on the path of achieving an education became a relentless urge. In retrospect, we can point to the Revolution for inspiring and igniting within us a quest to further our education. Many moved from the Wharf to board rooms, school rooms, and the chambers of law. Professionals in other fields, no longer following blindly an ideology, but pursuing dreams of our own with eyes wide opened.

Sir Eric Matthew Gairy and Herbert Preudhomme

The Night 1500 Carroll Street Kitchen Closed

1500 CARROLL STREET was not a refugee camp, but it was a place of refuge. The original Carroll Street crew came from the same Wharf community. Over the years, however, other relationships developed and they were joined by friends from other parts of Grenada and elsewhere. We survived the struggles and baggage of New York (Brooklyn in particular) because of our close bond and camaraderie spirit. We did not yield to the isms and schisms, vices and adventures that were responsible for leading others into the negatives to achieve the unreachable.

On any given weekend, the gatherings ranged from between fifteen to twenty-five male souls enjoying the cooking of Raul. There was not a dish Raul was incapable of putting together in five minutes, and everyone present ate well (a belly full), reminiscent of the biblical story of the five loafs and two fishes. We identified each other by the doorbell rings and expected punctuality from those who showed up once the pot was off the fire. My touch was three short blasts.

On Labor Day, Raul made available breakfast and lunch—enough for takeaway. The night that last pot came off the fire, we knew it was the end of an era. It was the "end of the lime" at 1500 Carroll Street.

About the author

CLEVROY "DEPO" DEPRADINE was born on the island of Grenada. Before immigrating to the United States in the mid-seventies, he was a member of the Panasonic Steel Orchestra and Angel Harps Steel Orchestra. The latter he captained from 1973 until 1976. In his early years, Depo attended the St.

George's Anglican Junior/Senior School (Hindsey). Later, New York City Technical College and Baruch College of New York. Prior to his retirement in 2015, he worked with the Grenada Consulate in New York, the Caribbean Tourism Organization (CTO) and the City of New York (Department of Social Services) as an Eligibility Specialist, then assistant to the Brooklyn/Manhattan deputy regional manager of the 'Family Assistance Program' (FIA).